Learning Qlik® Sense

The Official Guide

Get to grips with the vision of Qlik Sense for next generation business intelligence and data discovery

Christopher Ilacqua

Henric Cronström

James Richardson

BIRMINGHAM - MUMBAI

Learning Qlik® Sense
The Official Guide

First published: February 2015

Production reference: 1040215

Published by Packt Publishing Ltd.
Livery Place
35 Livery Street
Birmingham B3 2PB, UK.

ISBN 978-1-78217-335-9

www.packtpub.com

Credits

Authors
Christopher Ilacqua
Henric Cronström
James Richardson

Reviewer
Arthur Lee

Commissioning Editor
Akram Hussain

Acquisition Editors
Joanne Fitzpatrick
Sam Wood

Content Development Editor
Sam Wood

Technical Editor
Amit Ramadas

Copy Editors
Vikrant Phadke
Adithi Shetty

Proofreaders
Simran Bhogal
Paul Hindle

Indexer
Monica Ajmera Mehta

Production Coordinator
Arvindkumar Gupta

Cover Work
Arvindkumar Gupta

About the Authors

Dr. Christopher Ilacqua is the Research Director, Product Validation at Qlik®. He has been working with leading customers and partners in the U.S. for more than 3 years garnering feedback on Qlik Sense. Chris has over 25 years of experience in the field of planning and business intelligence, and he has established himself as a leading expert by advising, designing, and implementing hundreds of planning and business intelligence applications. He has a Doctorate in Business Administration, a Master's degree in Business Administration in Accounting, and a Bachelor's degree in Marketing. His research interests focus on big data, data governance, mobile BI, SaaS, business collaboration, and cloud-based solutions. Additionally, Chris serves as an adjunct professor at New England College of Business, where he teaches graduate students Strategic Leadership, Marketing, Operations Management, and MIS.

Dr. Henric Cronström is Vice President Product and Technical Product Advocate at Qlik®, where he has worked for most of the time since the company was founded. At Qlik, Henric has had several different roles. For the first few years in Qlik's history, he was the Product Manager for QlikView, and then he moved into solution implementation and training. After many years in the field, including a role as a manager for the technical staff in QlikTech, Germany, he returned to Sweden as Deputy Manager for the development organization. In his current role, his main task is the communication of technical products, on blogs, in the press, and directly with large accounts.

Henric has a Doctorate in Elementary Particle Physics from Lund University.

James Richardson is Business Analytics Strategist at Qlik®. Prior to joining Qlik, James spent 6 years as a Gartner analyst covering business intelligence and analytics. During his tenure, along with advising hundreds of organizations on BI topics, James was the lead author of the Magic Quadrant for BI Platforms report and was the chairperson and keynote speaker for Gartner's European BI summit. Before Gartner, James spent 13 years at BI and performance management software vendor IMRS/Arbor/Hyperion in various roles. Prior to that, James worked for Sema Group developing software for industrial control systems (SCADA), and as an advertising copywriter.

Acknowledgments

As with any project of this size, there are a number of people who helped support this book. First of all, we would like to thank Anthony Deighton and Donald Farmer for their vision of Qlik® Sense and their executive support for this project. Additionally, we would like to thank Arthur Lee and the Product Management team at Qlik who supported the technical review of this book.

We would also like to thank all the Qlik employees that joined us over the last 3 years at customer sites to help solicit feedback on Qlik Sense. These people include Jodi Antoni, Pierce Barber, Adrian Bereanu, Chris Brennan, Sean Donovan, Jeff DeAngelis, Dan English, Vinay Kapoor, Terry Kavouras, Mark Latessa, Arthur Lee, Erik Lövquist, Kevin Schulz, and Elif Tutuk. Thank you for sharing your time, knowledge of Qlik products, and customers. This book could not have been written without the hundreds of hours of conversations with customers and partners.

The last four chapters of this book are based on the hard work of the Qlik Demo team. These applications and new approaches to solve these business problems were created by Michael Anthony, Chuck Bannon, Alexander Karlsson, Jennell McIntire, Apeksha Patak, and Arturo Muñoz. Thank you for allowing us to bring life to your applications in this book.

Additionally, we wish to thank the Qlik legal team of Deborah Lofton, Alice Hume, and Heather Rossman for creating the legal framework that allowed us to explore Qlik Sense concepts with customers and partners. Also, we wish to thank the Social Influence and Reputation Management team of Maria Scurry and Toni Iafrate for their support and helping get the word out both internally and externally on the value of this project.

Finally and most importantly, we would also like to thank the companies who have contributed their time, resources, feedback, and passion for Qlik products for more than 3 years, which helped uncover the value of Qlik Sense in their organizations.

About the Reviewer

Arthur Lee has been Vice President of Product Management at Qlik® since June 2014. He has had various Qlik product management roles since joining Qlik in 2010. He is responsible for the Product Management function at Qlik. He has served as a business unit executive at IBM's Business Analytics business unit as a product manager among a variety of other product marketing roles at IBM Cognos TM1 from October 2004 to January 2010. Prior to IBM, he had several financial and consulting roles within banks, retail, and software companies.

Arthur holds a BA in Finance and Marketing from Boston College, Massachusetts.

www.packtpub.com

Support files, eBooks, discount offers, and more

For support files and downloads related to your book, please visit www.PacktPub.com.

Did you know that Packt offers eBook versions of every book published, with PDF and ePub files available? You can upgrade to the eBook version at www.packtpub.com and as a print book customer, you are entitled to a discount on the eBook copy. Get in touch with us at service@packtpub.com for more details.

At www.PacktPub.com, you can also read a collection of free technical articles, sign up for a range of free newsletters and receive exclusive discounts and offers on Packt books and eBooks.

https://www2.packtpub.com/books/subscription/packtlib

Do you need instant solutions to your IT questions? PacktLib is Packt's online digital book library. Here, you can search, access, and read Packt's entire library of books.

Why subscribe?

- Fully searchable across every book published by Packt
- Copy and paste, print, and bookmark content
- On demand and accessible via a web browser

Free access for Packt account holders

If you have an account with Packt at www.packtpub.com, you can use this to access PacktLib today and view 9 entirely free books. Simply use your login credentials for immediate access.

Instant updates on new Packt books

Get notified! Find out when new books are published by following @PacktEnterprise on Twitter or the *Packt Enterprise* Facebook page.

Table of Contents

Preface

Welcome! The purpose of this book is to help you learn about Qlik® Sense and Qlik®'s self-service visualization platform. Our aim is to help you get more from your data by applying Qlik Sense and its unique capabilities to your analytic needs. At the beginning of this book, we'll cover why Qlik chose to develop Qlik Sense, what data discovery is and can do, and the strategy and vision behind the product. In the subsequent chapters, we'll address practical considerations, including the Qlik Sense application life cycle, how to meet the needs of different types of users, how to develop and administer engaging Qlik Sense applications, data modeling, and getting the most out of the QIX engine. This book concludes by outlining a series of example applications built using Qlik Sense, to address analysis needs in sales management, HR, management, and demographics.

What this book covers

Chapter 1, Why Develop Qlik Sense?, covers why Qlik chose to develop Qlik Sense, what data discovery is and can do, and the strategy and vision behind the product.

Chapter 2, What is Data Discovery?, covers the fundamental difference between traditional business intelligence and data discovery, and how it facilitates users who need this information in their daily work.

Chapter 3, The Vision of Qlik Sense, covers the vision informing Qlik Sense, and the evolving requirements that are compeling organizations to readdress how they deliver business intelligence and support data-driven decision-making.

Chapter 4, Overview of a Qlik Sense Application's Life Cycle, covers the Qlik Sense application life cycle overview as a backdrop to highlight key features and benefits of Qlik Sense. There are thousands of features in Qlik Sense, and this chapter will serve as a guide to the major components, features, and benefits to start your exploration of the software.

Chapter 5, Empowering Next Generation Data Discovery Consumers, highlights key features in the context of specific requirements that Qlik has identified as a consumer.

Chapter 6, Contributing to Data Discovery, highlights key features in the context of specific user requirements that Qlik has identified as a contributor, or someone who seeks to share key findings from their analysis.

Chapter 7, Creating Engaging Applications, shows you how to build engaging applications to meet your business problems.

Chapter 8, Administering Qlik Sense, covers the administration of Qlik Sense applications within an organization.

Chapter 9, Sales Discovery, shows how to apply Qlik Sense to the challenges of analyzing sales performance within your organization.

Chapter 10, Human Resource Discovery, guides you through applying Qlik Sense to the challenges of analyzing human resource data.

Chapter 11, Travel Expense Discovery, takes us through applying Qlik Sense to the challenges of analyzing travel expense management within an organization.

Chapter 12, Demographic Data Discovery, ends the book by demonstrating how Qlik Sense can be applied to the challenges of analyzing demographic data.

What you need for this book

You can begin your exploration of Qlik Sense with a copy of Qlik Sense Desktop, which is available for free at `http://www.qlik.com/us/explore/products/sense/desktop`. Additionally, the sample applications' examples and many others are available for you to explore live at `http://sense-demo.qlik.com/`. Please bookmark this link as additional demonstrations and examples are constantly being added and updated. Additionally, this book covers a broad range of topics that are available only through Qlik Sense. Please contact your local Qlik account executive for additional information.

Who this book is for

If you are looking for an intuitive way to analyze data through Qlik Sense and make better business decisions, this is the book for you. This can include casual users who are looking for an easy product that helps them understand their data and helps transform their data into actionable information. Additionally, this book provides information for analysts, authors, and administrators who seek to help organizations improve the performance of decision-making across their organization through Qlik Sense.

Conventions

In this book, you will find a number of text styles that distinguish between different kinds of information. Here are some examples of these styles and an explanation of their meaning.

Code words in text, database table names, folder names, filenames, file extensions, pathnames, dummy URLs, user input, and Twitter handles are shown as follows: "The Budget table contains all the key information."

New terms and **important words** are shown in bold. Words that you see on the screen, for example, in menus or dialog boxes, appear in the text like this: "Before we begin, let's review the main sheets within the **Travel Expense Management** application."

 Warnings or important notes appear in a box like this.

Reader feedback

Feedback from our readers is always welcome. Let us know what you think about this book—what you liked or disliked. Reader feedback is important for us as it helps us develop titles that you will really get the most out of.

To send us general feedback, simply e-mail feedback@packtpub.com, and mention the book's title in the subject of your message.

If there is a topic that you have expertise in and you are interested in either writing or contributing to a book, see our author guide at www.packtpub.com/authors.

Customer support

Now that you are the proud owner of a Packt book, we have a number of things to help you to get the most from your purchase.

Reviewing the example applications

The examples and many others are available for you to explore live at http://sense-demo.qlik.com/. Please bookmark this link as additional demonstrations and examples are constantly being added and updated.

Downloading the color images of this book

We also provide you with a PDF file that has color images of the screenshots/diagrams used in this book. The color images will help you better understand the changes in the output. You can download this file from `https://www.packtpub.com/sites/default/files/downloads/3359EN_ColoredImages.pdf`.

Errata

Although we have taken every care to ensure the accuracy of our content, mistakes do happen. If you find a mistake in one of our books—maybe a mistake in the text or the code—we would be grateful if you could report this to us. By doing so, you can save other readers from frustration and help us improve subsequent versions of this book. If you find any errata, please report them by visiting `http://www.packtpub.com/submit-errata`, selecting your book, clicking on the **Errata Submission Form** link, and entering the details of your errata. Once your errata are verified, your submission will be accepted and the errata will be uploaded to our website or added to any list of existing errata under the Errata section of that title.

To view the previously submitted errata, go to `https://www.packtpub.com/books/content/support` and enter the name of the book in the search field. The required information will appear under the **Errata** section.

Piracy

Piracy of copyrighted material on the Internet is an ongoing problem across all media. At Packt, we take the protection of our copyright and licenses very seriously. If you come across any illegal copies of our works in any form on the Internet, please provide us with the location address or website name immediately so that we can pursue a remedy.

Please contact us at `copyright@packtpub.com` with a link to the suspected pirated material.

We appreciate your help in protecting our authors and our ability to bring you valuable content.

Questions

If you have a problem with any aspect of this book, you can contact us at `questions@packtpub.com`, and we will do our best to address the problem.

1
Why Develop Qlik Sense?

In this chapter, we'll start getting to grips with what Qlik® Sense offers by getting a better understanding of Qlik's background and how Qlik Sense came to be developed. We will cover the following topics:

- Qlik's history in business intelligence
- The evolution of data discovery
- The QlikView.Next project
- The increased business demands for data analysis

A history of disruption

In the world of technology, there's a lot of talk about creating new products that disrupt existing markets, but very few organizations can say they've done it for real. Qlik is one of them.

In 2007, the **business intelligence (BI)** software market changed forever. Oracle bought Hyperion, SAP bought Business Objects, and IBM bought Cognos. The conventional wisdom was that BI would effectively cease to exist as a standalone market, subsumed into larger stacks of technology.

However, this wasn't the case. In fact, by 2007, a revolution was already well underway. The BI world was being fundamentally disrupted, challenged by the new approach pioneered by Qlik (then called QlikTech). The disruptive technology Qlik developed was called QlikView®. To differentiate QlikView from the established BI products, Qlik began to call the new disruptive approach **Business Discovery**, later adopting **data discovery** as this term gained industry-wide adoption.

Surprisingly though, when it launched in 1994, what became QlikView was not consciously targeted at the BI software market. Rather, its initial task was to help its first customer understand which of a number of individual parts and manufacturing materials were used across the range of the complex machines it manufactured, and which parts were *not* associated with particular items (a critical point we'll explore in *Chapter 2, What is Data Discovery?* and revisit throughout this book). The goal was to visualize the logical relations between the parts, materials, machines, and products. This origin led to an approach completely different from BI at the time, one in which all associated data points are linked automatically, enabling discoveries to be made through free exploration of data.

As it became more widely used and deployed, it was evident that what QlikView was being used for was a new type of BI. QlikView's speed, usability, and relevance challenged the standard approach that was dominated by IT-deployed data reporting products, which are slow performing, hard to use, and built around models that struggle to keep up with the pace of modern business needs.

QlikView's intuitive visual user interface, patented associative data handling—running entirely in memory—and its capability to draw data together from disparate sources changed the landscape. Discovery-led BI is about giving people the power to interact with and explore data in a much more valuable way than the older, reporting-led BI incumbency could. This is massively compelling to people who need to quickly ask and answer questions based on data in order to learn and make decisions, and proved very compelling to people jaded with the way things had been done before.

Rethinking data discovery

So what does Qlik do now? Sit back and relax, proud of its disruptive chops? Safe in the knowledge that it's recast an established market in its image? No. Far from it. Instead, Qlik took the decision to try and transform the BI market again with a new product. The challenge though is that in doing so, it must also disrupt itself.

Why should we do this? Why did we decide to build **Qlik Sense**?

The company culture

The first reason is that Qlik's culture, informed by its Swedish roots—the company was founded in the Lund University, Sweden—is restless and questioning. Qlik is driven by the desire to design better ways for people to use information. The company wants to build analytic software that is easy, elegant, and natural to use, bringing computing power to bear on complex data. To do so, it needed to develop a new product that goes beyond the scope of its original product idea.

Competitive changes

The second reason to build Qlik Sense is increased competition. Given the success of discovery-led BI, look-alike QlikView mimics are multiplying. The software titans are reworking their BI efforts to emulate Qlik's value proposition and might soon offer a "good enough" simulacrum at a low price point. "Good enough" is very dangerous because mega vendors are willing to give "good enough" away for free. Further, Qlik now also has its own group of fast-follower competitors; firms that focus on one area of the functionality offered by QlikView, often data visualization, and offer compelling capabilities in this narrow area alone. These competitive changes meant that Qlik could not be complacent about its product strengths.

The third and arguably most important reason to build Qlik Sense was the knowledge that if Qlik didn't disrupt itself, a new competitor might. No organization can forestall the arrival of a black swan. The best way to minimize the chance of one appearing on the horizon is to become a competitor yourself. To do so takes courage because it means taking a hard look at the company's established products and having a frank understanding of the external situation that defines how any new product might be used.

Market dynamics

This type of critical thinking led Qlik to the realization that what people want from discovery-led BI is changing as the availability and mix of analytic technology skills develops.

Although loved by users, the main QlikView value proposition was really based on its ability to speed up developers' work, giving people the ability to build useful BI apps when needed by business decision-makers. When it came to this type of agility, Qlik was unique and unmatched. Although now things have changed, data-savvy authors, who want to build analytic apps, have a large number of simple, and in many cases free, toolsets to choose from: visualization libraries such as D3 to full application development toolsets such as .NET, Ruby, and web UI programming frameworks such jQuery and Prototype. Many of these toolkits are available on an open source basis and are helpful to create interactive, visual, and data-driven user experiences. Further, the use and capabilities of these developer tools is growing. As such, Qlik's product authors realized that any new product had to provide a standard, simple, and open application development framework in order to fit better into today's technical environment.

Further, the new product had to extend user-driven capabilities to an unheard of level. In the 20 years since QlikView was invented, people's expectations of technology have shifted based on their experience as consumers. BI technology has to meet these needs, providing an immersive, immediately accessible experience that functions on their device of choice instantly. The whole idea of data discovery is putting power in the hands of every user. The new product had to be barrier-free when it came to adoption. For example, anyone using it had to be able to make sense of an application that a developer built easily; or add a much-needed chart to an existing app; or, bring data into a Qlik Sense to build a simple app with no prelearning required.

The QlikView.Next project

Given these points, Qlik took the decision to disrupt itself and the market again. It decided to design and develop a next generation data discovery platform. Developed under the project name QlikView.Next and launched as Qlik Sense, the product was anchored to five themes:

- **Gorgeous and genius**: Within this theme Qlik focused on three product scenarios, with an overall emphasis on ad hoc analysis. The scenarios were that the product should be visually beautiful, support associative, comparative, and anticipatory analysis, and offer *one client to rule them all*—a seamless experience across all devices.

- **Mobility with agility**: This theme was about all users having access and the ability to answer new analytical questions as they arise in new situations and contexts when using a mobile device, with no difference between static and mobile experiences.

- **Compulsive collaboration**: Business intelligence and collaboration are inseparable; decision-making is, by nature, a collaborative activity. The intent was to build a product that could reside at the forefront of users' shared decision-making and give them the chance to communicate their insights through collaboration and storytelling.

- **The premier platform**: This theme was about enabling Qlik customers and partners to quickly and easily deliver apps and solutions that are perfectly relevant to their constituents. Within this theme, Qlik focused on four scenarios: data access, the development experience, expanding its ecosystem through broadened APIs, and offering a unified platform interface.

- **Enabling new enterprise**: With this theme, Qlik was focused on making capabilities such as security, reliability, and scalability available to all customers, not just the largest ones, and giving administrators and authors the same kind of gorgeous and genius experience other users get.

Making sense of modern business

You may say, "Well, that's all good but it doesn't really tell me why this matters or why Qlik Sense is important."

To answer this, we have to think about what the focus of technology in our organizations has been in the recent past. For 25 years, most of our investment in IT has been on effectively improving reliability, using ERP or transactional applications to streamline processes, drive out inefficiencies, and deliver our products or services effectively. However, if most organizations, and particularly groups of competitors, are now operating at similar levels of procedural effectiveness, a key question arises: what do we do differently to win?

The answer lies in out-thinking our competitors through the use of data and analysis. This requires a shift of focus in both how we run our businesses and the IT world needed to do so. So far, analytics has too often been a poor cousin, something that happens afterwards on the edges, a tactical rather than strategic activity. That's no longer good enough. Businesses using data-driven decision-making perform measurably better than those that don't. When we can see (and measure) new things, we are driven to seek answers and thus, new ways of thinking and operating. Organizations that do not have analytics as a central part of their business activities will not thrive or even survive in the new reality.

Qlik Sense is about doing exactly that; freeing up the analytic skills of individuals in organizations, whatever their role. This book shows you how to make the most of that and alter how your organization uses information.

Summary

In this chapter, we looked at the internal company and external market drivers that prompted Qlik to develop Qlik Sense. We've also considered the aims the company set itself for the new product, and why that's so important in today's business environment. In the next chapter, we'll cover the new style of BI that Qlik pioneered, data discovery, in more detail.

What is Data Discovery?

2

We've seen how the BI market is changing rapidly and how new demands have transformed the way that users look at analysis. In this chapter, we will examine the new discovery-based approach to business intelligence, which is rapidly emerging and has defined Qlik® Sense.

In this chapter, we will cover the following topics:

- The Qlik® philosophy
- The approach to data discovery
- The importance of the empowered user
- How a user *really* interacts with data
- The difference between traditional BI and data discovery

Why do we need data discovery?

Over the years, there have been many names of the different business intelligence methods and tools, such as:

- Executive Information Systems (EIS)
- Management Information Systems (MIS)
- Online Analytical Processing (OLAP)
- Decision Support Systems (DSS)
- Management reporting
- Ad hoc query and reporting

Do we really need an additional label for something that in principle is the same thing? The answer is yes.

There is a fundamental difference between older technologies and data discovery, and it is in the approach. Most of the preceding tools are oriented towards technology, but data discovery is not. Instead, data discovery is oriented towards people—towards the users who need the information in their daily work.

Most of the preceding tools were developed for a small, select number of decision-makers, but again, data discovery is not. Data discovery is for everyone.

Decisions are made at all levels in a company. Obviously, managers are decision-makers, but we sometimes forget that machine operators and receptionists are also decision-makers, albeit at a more local level. They also need information to make better decisions.

We, at Qlik, believe that information can change the world and that every user can contribute to this transformation. Everyone should easily be able to view data, navigate in data, and analyze data. Everyone should be able to experience that "a-ha" moment of discovery.

Data discovery is not just business intelligence. It is user-centric, dynamic, and empowering. And it is fun!

The empowered user

For the first couple of years in Qlik's history, the company was called QuikTech and the product was called QuikView. It was a game with words: the product name insinuated that you could view things quickly, and at the same time, the letters Q-U-I-K were an abbreviation for what we believed in: **Quality**, **Understanding**, **Information**, and **Knowledge**. These are shown in the following banner:

 Quality - Understanding - Information - Knowledge

The initial QuikTech banner

Qlik believed that a business could improve its processes and product quality by empowering employees and encouraging them to engage in lifelong learning. And Qlik meant *all* employees—we saw everyone as a decision-maker, not just managers.

To get information from data was an important part of creating understanding, knowledge, and quality. We were inspired by the management trends of the time, especially by employee empowerment as described in the book, *Moments of Truth* by *Jan Carlzon* (President and CEO of Scandinavian Airlines), *HarperBusiness* (Swedish: Riv pyramiderna!).

Thus, the abbreviation was an early attempt to make a statement on values and it was there long before the genesis of the product. What the abbreviation stood for was really the ideological base when founding the company.

The company later changed its name to QlikTech, and the values statement was adjusted accordingly to look like what is shown in the following banner:

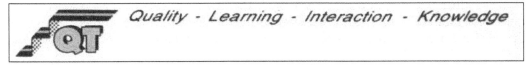

Quality - Learning - Interaction - Knowledge

The second QlikTech banner

Today Qlik's mission statement is "Simplifying Decisions for Everyone, Everywhere". The words we use to describe our mission have changed slightly, from the general "Knowledge" and "Quality" to the more specific "Decisions", which is the main step in converting knowledge to quality.

The current mission statement is more to the point than our original values statement. Further, it includes the idea that all people are included, which is something we took for granted but failed to express in our initial values statement. In all aspects, the current mission statement is a very good description of what we stood for 20 years ago and what we still stand for today.

Although some things have changed since then, much remains the same: users are still often in a situation where they are unable to analyze their data—data that they have the right to see, or should have the right to see, in order to do a good job. Rigid systems, technical limitations, and poor user interfaces are usually the culprits.

However, people's expectations of software have changed dramatically during the last decade. Applications from Google and Apple invite users to interact with simple, friendly interfaces. Search bars, Like buttons, and touchscreens have transformed the way people explore, consume, and share information. Today, people want the same ease of use from their business tools as they get from their consumer tools at home.

The current trends such as the consumerization of software, performance improvements of hardware, usability improvements of software, mobile devices, social networks, and so on just accelerate this change. All these trends are reshaping user behavior. Yesterday, a user was a passive end user, but the user of tomorrow will be both able and demanding. They will demand tools that are fast, flexible, and dynamic. They will demand tools that they can use themselves. The empowered user is here to stay.

The interaction with data

The classic picture of business intelligence is that the user has one or several questions, and that the data holds the answers. So the problem boils down to creating a tool where the user can enter their questions, and the tool can return the answers.

However, this picture is incorrect. The truth is that the user does not always know the question initially. Or rather, if the user knows the question, they often already know the answer. So, the first thing the tool should do is to help the user find the questions.

Finding the questions is a process that involves exploring the data. It involves testing what you suspect but don't know for sure. It also involves discovering new facts. Further, it involves playing with data, turning it around, scrutinizing the facts, and formulating a possible question. You use your gut feeling as a source of ideas and you use the data to refine the ideas into knowledge; or to discard the ideas, if facts show that the ideas are wrong. You need to be able to play with the data, to turn facts around and look at them from different angles before you can say that you understand the data, and you need to understand the data before you can talk smartly about it.

When you have found a relevant question, you also need to be able to conduct an analysis to get a well-founded answer to the question.

Finally, the process involves presenting the answer to the question to other people as a basis for a decision or an action. The tool must support the entire process of going from ignorance to insight.

Hence, one major difference between data discovery and the more old-fashioned tools is that data discovery software supports the entire process—the process of coming from a blank mind, not knowing what you are looking for, all the way to attaining knowledge and taking action.

This is what data discovery is all about: helping you to prepare before you speak, act, or make a decision. It is the process of going from the darkness to the light, from the unknown to the known, from ignorance to insight. It is the process of going all the way from a blank mind to a substantiated argument.

The traditional business intelligence architecture

It is quite clear that users representing the business want the ability to ask and answer questions on their own so that they can make better decisions, but traditional business intelligence solutions aren't well-suited for user demands. Instead, it is common that the systems are created in a report-centric manner, where governance and system demands set the goals, rather than user demands. The solutions often have preconfigured dashboards, fixed drill-down paths, predefined queries, predefined views, and very little flexibility.

With traditional BI, the creation of the business intelligence solution often belongs to the IT organization, which has to do the following: create data models, establish a semantic layer, build reports and dashboards, and protect and control the data. Often, the creation of business intelligence solutions is not driven by user demands. The following figure depicts the traditional BI architecture:

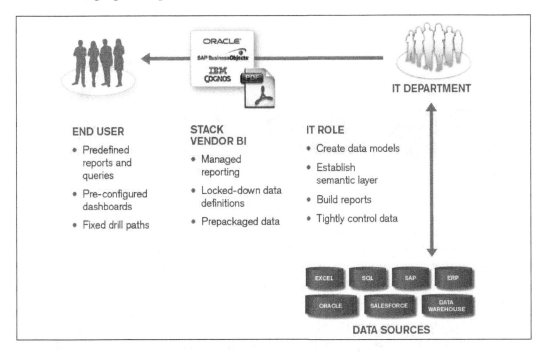

When analyzing data, you want to set filters so that you can make selections, but with traditional tools, you often need to start at the top of predefined hierarchies. So instead of selecting a customer directly, you may need to answer this question: which market does this customer belong to?, then its country, and only then can you specify the customer.

Further, in the drill-down hierarchy, you are often limited to the choice of one or all. For example, you can look at either a single customer or all of them. The possibility of choosing two or three specific customers doesn't exist, unless this has been specifically predefined by the data model developer.

Numbers are often precalculated to ensure short response times, but this has a drawback that if the developer hasn't anticipated a specific calculation, the tool will not be able to show it.

Further, the architecture of the tool is often made in three layers; the **stack**. The first layer is the **Extract, Transform, Load** (ETL) layer, or the data load layer. The second is the **Data Store / Engine** layer, and the third is the **User Interface** (UI) layer. The three layers are different pieces of software, sometimes delivered by different software vendors.

These three layers also demand different skillsets. Often the ETL expert knows little or nothing about the UI software, and the UI expert knows little or nothing about the ETL.

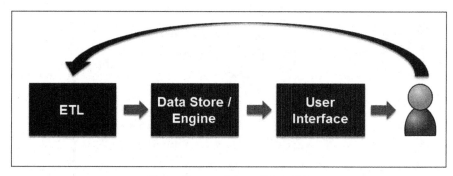

The product stack in traditional BI

This architecture also leads to problems. When an application is built, the feedback comes from users trying to use the application. It could be that KPIs are incorrectly calculated or that dimensions or measures are missing. It could also mean that the user realizes that the initial requirements were incorrect or insufficient. The feedback could imply changes in the UI, or in the data model, or even in the ETL component.

This type of feedback is normal — it happens with all business intelligence tools. It only means that the development of applications is a process where you need to be agile and prepared. The expectation that you should be able to define an application completely and correctly prior to a prototype or an intermediate version is just unrealistic.

This is where the architecture leads to problems. In order for a project to be successful, you need to be able to implement change requests and new user demands with short notice, and this is extremely difficult since three different pieces of software and three different groups of people are involved. The distance between the user and the ETL component is just too great for efficient communication. Hence, traditional architecture leads to a broken process.

The Qlik way

Qlik has tried to solve all the drawbacks discussed in the preceding section by doing things differently.

First of all, you click and view. You don't need to formulate your question or tell the system more specifically what you want to look at. You just click, and by that, you say "Tell me more about that...". Then you look at the calculation, KPI, or field that might be interesting.

Color coding

The color coding defines the answer. Some things are associated with what you clicked on, and they remain white. Others that are not associated become gray. The color coding is for simplicity. The user quickly gets an overview and understands how things work.

Showing the excluded reveals the unexpected, creates insight, and creates new questions. Hence, the gray color is an important part of making the Qlik experience an associative one—a data dialog and an information interaction—rather than just a database query. Showing you that something is excluded when you didn't expect it means answering questions you didn't ask. This surprise creates new knowledge in a way that only a true data discovery platform can.

Freedom of data navigation

A user has total freedom to navigate through data and make any combination of selections. Any number of values can be selected. No drill-down paths need to be predefined. This allows the user to follow their own train of thought instead of someone else's. Start anywhere and just follow your intuition.

This total freedom when exploring data is really the core attribute of data discovery.

Calculation on demand

Further, no numbers need to be precalculated. QlikView® and Qlik® Sense calculate everything on demand, usually in a fraction of a second. The short response time allows the user to "have a conversation" with the data, where one answer leads to the next question, which in turn leads to next, and so on. Only this way can you interact with data so that you learn from it.

The developer does not need to anticipate all questions that the user will pose. All they need to do is to create a logical, coherent data model, and Qlik Sense will be able to answer the question correctly:

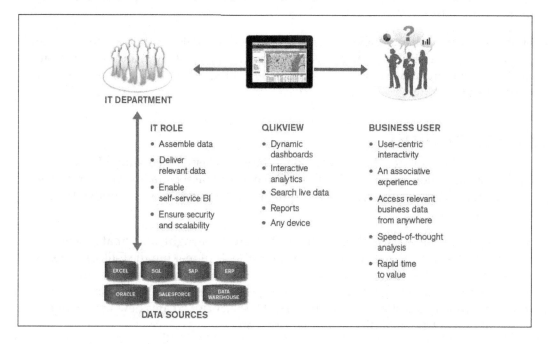

The stack (ETL-Data Store / Engine-UI) is replaced by a single integrated environment. This makes it possible to develop applications in close cooperation with the users, and it can often be done by the users themselves. Feedback is implemented instantaneously and the changes can be evaluated just seconds later. This shortens the development cycle and ensures that the application meets the user demands much sooner than it would otherwise.

This step-wise implementation is crucial for the success of a business intelligence project. It is also the core of modern agile methodologies that are used in all types of software development.

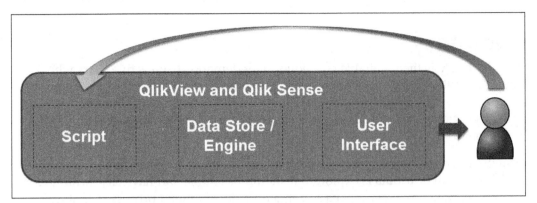

With Qlik Sense, all BI stack functions are integrated into one tool

Development of business intelligence applications must be done as close to the user as possible to enable user feedback and short development cycles. It does not necessarily imply self-service capability, although it is good if this capability exists.

With the introduction of Qlik Sense, the ground-breaking work continues by enabling a new class of users who are highly mobile and require greater self-service capabilities. In Qlik Sense, the self-service capability has become a core feature. Users can define new graphs and visualizations that the app developer didn't think of. This functionality empowers the users even further.

With Qlik Sense, it has also become easier to share your findings and communicate them. This is something that is necessary in all environments where human interaction is important, which is pretty much everywhere.

Data discovery – the next generation of BI

Data discovery is the future of business intelligence. With data discovery, users pursue their own path to insight, make discoveries collaboratively, and can arrive at a whole new level of decision-making. Users are not limited to predefined paths or precalculated numbers. They do not need to formulate questions ahead of time. They can interact with data, find the questions, ask what they need to ask, and explore up, down, and sideways rather than only drilling down in a predefined hierarchy.

Organizations may still need standardized reporting for many cases, but data discovery is the approach that ultimately fulfills the promise of business intelligence for everyone.

Summary

Data discovery is the inevitable consequence of demands from active users who want information from the ever-increasing amount of data. From the very beginning, the core of the Qlik philosophy was the empowered user. It affects both the view of how BI solutions should be developed and how the user interface of the tool should be designed.

In summary, data discovery is user-centric; it is BI for the empowered user. It means total freedom in how data is explored. It should be simple and have as few limitations as possible. Data discovery means a user-centric development process so that user feedback can be implemented instantaneously.

In the next chapter, we will look some of the other factors behind the development of Qlik Sense.

3
The Vision of Qlik Sense

In this chapter, we will look at the evolving requirements that compel organizations to readdress how they deliver business intelligence and support data-driven decision-making. This is important as it supplies some of the reasons as to why Qlik® Sense is relevant and important to their success. The purpose of covering these factors is so that you can consider and plan for them in your organization. Among other things, in this chapter, we will cover the following topics:

- The ongoing data explosion
- The rise of in-memory processing
- Barrierless BI through Human-Computer Interaction
- The consumerization of BI and the rise of self-service
- The use of information as an asset
- The changing role of IT

Evolving market factors

Technologies are developed and evolved in response to the needs of the environment they are created and used within. The most successful new technologies anticipate upcoming changes in order to help people take advantage of altered circumstances or reimagine how things are done. Any market is defined by both the suppliers—in this case, Qlik®—and the buyers, that is, the people who want to get more use and value from their information. Buyers' wants and needs are driven by a variety of macro and micro factors, and these are always in flux in some markets more than others. This is obviously and apparently the case in the world of data, BI, and analytics, which has been changing at a great pace due to a number of factors discussed further in the rest of this chapter. Qlik Sense has been designed to be the means through which organizations and the people that are a part of them thrive in a changed environment.

Big, big, and even bigger data

A key factor is that there's simply much more data in many forms to analyze than before. We're in the middle of an ongoing, accelerating data boom. According to Science Daily, 90 percent of the world's data was generated over the past two years. The fact is that with technologies such as Hadoop and NoSQL databases, we now have unprecedented access to cost-effective data storage. With vast amounts of data now storable and available for analysis, people need a way to sort the signal from the noise. People from a wider variety of roles—not all of them BI users or business analysts—are demanding better, greater access to data, regardless of where it comes from. Qlik Sense's fundamental design centers on bringing varied data together for exploration in an easy and powerful way.

The slow spinning down of the disk

At the same time, we are seeing a shift in how computation occurs and potentially, how information is managed. Fundamentals of the computing architectures that we've used for decades, the spinning disk and moving read head, are becoming outmoded. This means storing and accessing data has been around since Edison invented the cylinder phonograph in 1877. It's about time this changed. This technology has served us very well; it was elegant and reliable, but it has limitations. Speed limitations primarily.

Fundamentals that we take for granted today in BI, such as relational and multidimensional storage models, were built around these limitations. So were our IT skills, whether we realized it at the time. With the use of in-memory processing and 64-bit addressable memory spaces, these limitations are gone! This means a complete change in how we think about analysis. Processing data in memory means we can do analysis that was impractical or impossible before with the old approach. With in-memory computing, analysis that would've taken days before, now takes just seconds (or much less). However, why does it matter? Because it allows us to use the time more effectively; after all, time is the most finite resource of all. In-memory computing enables us to ask more questions, test more scenarios, do more experiments, debunk more hypotheses, explore more data, and run more simulations in the short window available to us. For IT, it means no longer trying to second-guess what users will do months or years in advance and trying to premodel it in order to achieve acceptable response times. People hate watching the hourglass spin.

Qlik Sense's predecessor QlikView® was built on the exploitation of in-memory processing; Qlik Sense has it at its core too.

Ubiquitous computing and the Internet of Things

You may know that more than a billion people use Facebook, but did you know that the majority of those people do so from a mobile device? The growth in the number of devices connected to the Internet is absolutely astonishing. According to Cisco's Zettabyte Era report, Internet traffic from wireless devices will exceed traffic from wired devices in 2014.

If we were writing this chapter even as recently as a year ago, we'd probably be talking about mobile BI as a separate thing from desktop or laptop delivered analytics. The fact of the matter is that we've quickly gone beyond that. For many people now, the most common way to use technology is on a mobile device, and they expect the kind of experience they've become used to on their iOS or Android device to be mirrored in complex software, such as the technology they use for visual discovery and analytics.

From its inception, Qlik Sense has had mobile usage in the center of its design ethos. It's the first data discovery software to be built for mobiles, and that's evident in how it uses HTML5 to automatically render output for the device being used, whatever it is. Plug in a laptop running Qlik Sense to a 70-inch OLED TV and the visual output is resized and re-expressed to optimize the new form factor.

So mobile is the new normal. This may be astonishing but it's just the beginning. Mobile technology isn't just a medium to deliver information to people, but an acceleration of data production for analysis too. By 2020, pretty much everyone and an increasing number of things will be connected to the Internet. There are 7 billion people on the planet today. Intel predicts that by 2020, more than 31 billion devices will be connected to the Internet. So, that's not just devices used by people directly to consume or share information. More and more things will be put online and communicate their state: cars, fridges, lampposts, shoes, rubbish bins, pets, plants, heating systems—you name it.

These devices will generate a huge amount of data from sensors that monitor all kinds of measurable attributes: temperature, velocity, direction, orientation, and time. This means an increasing opportunity to understand a huge gamut of data, but without the right technology and approaches it will be complex to analyze what is going on. Old methods of analysis won't work, as they don't move quickly enough. The variety and volume of information that can be analyzed will explode at an exponential rate. The rise of this type of big data makes us redefine how we build, deliver, and even promote analytics. It is an opportunity for those organizations that can exploit it through analysis; this can sort the signals from the noise and make sense of the patterns in the data. Qlik Sense is designed as just such a signal booster; it takes how users can zoom and pan through information too large for them to easily understand the product.

Unbound Human-Computer Interaction

We touched on the boundary between the computing power and the humans using it in the previous section. Increasingly, we're removing barriers between humans and technology. Take the rise of touch devices. Users don't want to just view data presented to them in a static form. Instead, they want to "feel" the data and interact with it. The same is increasingly true of BI. The adoption of BI tools has been too low because the technology has been hard to use. Adoption has been low because in the past BI tools often required people to conform to the tool's way of working, rather than reflecting the users way of thinking.

The aspiration for Qlik Sense (when part of the QlikView.Next project) was that the software should be both "gorgeous and genius". The genius part obviously refers to the built-in intelligence, the smarts, the software will have. The gorgeous part is misunderstood or at least oversimplified. Yes, it means cosmetically attractive (which is important) but much more importantly, it means enjoyable to use and experience. In other words, Qlik Sense should never be jarring to users but seamless, perhaps almost transparent to them, inducing a state of mental flow that encourages thinking about the question being considered rather than the tool used to answer it. The aim was to be of most value to people. Qlik Sense will empower users to explore their data and uncover hidden insights, naturally.

Evolving customer requirements

It is not only the external market drivers that impact how we use information. Our organizations and the people that work within them are also changing in their attitude towards technology, how they express ideas through data, and how increasingly they make use of data as a competitive weapon.

Consumerization of BI and the rise of self-service

The consumerization of any technology space is all about how enterprises are affected by, and can take advantage of, new technologies and models that originate and develop in the consumer marker, rather than in the enterprise IT sector. The reality is that individuals react quicker than enterprises to changes in technology. As such, consumerization cannot be stopped, nor is it something to be adopted. It can be embraced. While it's not viable to build a BI strategy around consumerization alone, its impact must be considered.

Consumerization makes itself felt in three areas:

- **Technology**: Most investment in innovation occurs in the consumer space first, with enterprise vendors incorporating consumer-derived features after the fact. (Think about how vendors added the browser as a UI for business software applications.)

- **Economics**: Consumer offerings are often less expensive or free (to try) with a low barrier of entry. This drives prices down, including enterprise sectors, and alters selection behavior.

- **People**: Demographics, which is the flow of Millennial Generation into the workplace, and the blurring of home/work boundaries and roles, which may be seen from a traditional IT perspective as rogue users, with demands to BYOPC or device.

In line with consumerization, BI users want to be able to pick up and just use the technology to create and share engaging solutions; they don't want to read the manual. This places a high degree of importance on the **Human-Computer Interaction (HCI)** aspects of a BI product (refer to the preceding list) and governed access to information and deployment design. Add mobility to this and you get a brand new sourcing and adoption dynamic in BI, one that Qlik engendered, and Qlik Sense is designed to take advantage of. Think about how Qlik Sense Desktop was made available as a freemium offer.

Information as an asset and differentiator

As times change, so do differentiators. For example, car manufacturers in the 1980s differentiated themselves based on reliability, making sure their cars started every single time. Today, we expect that our cars will start; reliability is now a commodity. The same is true for ERP systems. Originally, companies implemented ERPs to improve reliability, but in today's post-ERP world, companies are shifting to differentiating their businesses based on information. This means our focus changes from apps to analytics. And analytics apps, like those delivered by Qlik Sense, help companies access the data they need to set themselves apart from the competition.

However, to get maximum return from information, the analysis must be delivered fast enough, and in sync with the operational tempo people need. Things are speeding up all the time. For example, take the fashion industry. Large mainstream fashion retailers used to work two seasons per year. Those that stuck to that were destroyed by fast fashion retailers. The same is true for old style, system-of-record BI tools; they just can't cope with today's demands for speed and agility.

The rise of information activism

A new, tech-savvy generation is entering the workforce, and their expectations are different than those of past generations. The Beloit College Mindset List for the entering class of 2017 gives the perspective of students entering college this year, how they see the world, and the reality they've known all their lives. For this year's freshman class, Java has never been just a cup of coffee and a tablet is no longer something you take in the morning. This new generation of workers grew up with the Internet and is less likely to be passive with data. They bring their own devices everywhere they go, and expect it to be easy to mash-up data, communicate, and collaborate with their peers.

The evolution and elevation of the role of IT

We've all read about how the role of IT is changing, and the question CIOs today must ask themselves is: "How do we drive innovation?". IT must transform from being gatekeepers (doers) to storekeepers (enablers), providing business users with self-service tools they need to be successful. However, to achieve this transformation, they need to stock helpful tools and provide consumable information products or apps. Qlik Sense is a key part of the armory that IT needs to provide to be successful in this transformation.

Summary

In this chapter, we looked at the factors that provide the wider context for the use of Qlik Sense. The factors covered arise out of both increasing technical capability and demands to compete in a globalized, information-centric world, where out-analyzing your competitors is a key success factor.

In the next chapter, we will look in detail at Qlik Sense itself and how its features and benefits help in meeting these requirements, beginning with the application's life cycle.

4
Overview of a Qlik Sense Application's Life Cycle

In the previous chapters, we outlined the evolving requirements driven by the market, and more importantly by business users seeking to help make better decisions within their organization. This chapter's goal is to highlight key features and benefits of Qlik Sense in meeting these requirements. There are thousands of features in the initial release of the software, and this chapter will serve as a guide to the major components, features, and benefits of Qlik Sense as you start exploring it.

In this chapter, we'll be covering the following topics:

- Overview of the hub
- Starting application authoring
- Components of a Qlik Sense application
- Sharing an application

Overview of an application's life cycle

As we begin our overview of a Qlik Sense application life cycle, it is best to start at the center of a Qlik Sense community collaboration, which is called the hub. The hub is made up of a number of streams that contain applications that are published by authors as well as users who can extend these applications by adding personal sheets and data stories. The **Qlik Sense Management Console** (**QMC**) governs this publishing through streams that have security rules. This approach provides the highly governed system that IT needs, while granting users the ability to explore information and share and collaborate on their findings.

Let's dig a bit deeper in each of these areas.

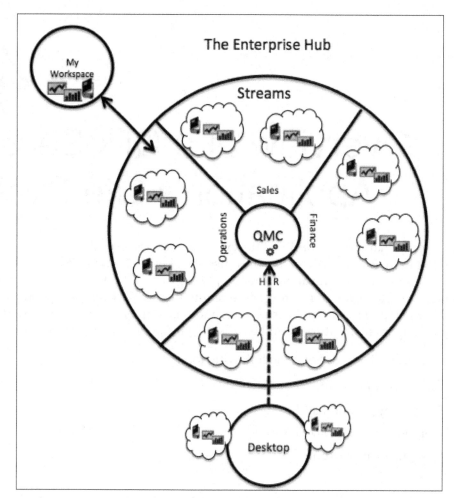

Overview of the Qlik Sense hub

Starting application authoring

The need for a Qlik Sense application often starts with simple questions, such
as these: why are sales down in my region? What products are not selling well?
Are there opportunities to sell additional products to existing customers? When
a customer buys a product, do they also purchase a companion product? These
types of questions lead to the identification of the place to find this data. Qlik Sense
provides two starting points that can be from either the Personal (Desktop) or
Enterprise Edition. This chapter will focus primarily on the Qlik Sense Enterprise
Edition and mention the differences in the Desktop Edition.

The hub is made up of two main parts. The first is **My Workspace**, which enables users to create new Qlik Sense applications. The second part comprises defined **Streams**, which contain published applications to be used and extended by users. Streams are defined in the QMC, which provides a broad range of security rules to meet organization requirements. The Desktop Edition contains only a hub for the creation of Qlik Sense applications. Once an application is completed, it can be published to an authorized stream by the author. When published, the application cannot be altered without republishing by the author. For the Desktop Edition, the application author must send all artifacts of the application, which must include at least the Qlik Sense document (QVF) and any images and extensions used in the development of the application. Once received by the administrator, these artifacts are imported through the QMC and then published.

What makes up a Qlik Sense application?

Now let's turn our attention to what components make up a Qlik Sense application. They are shown in the following diagram:

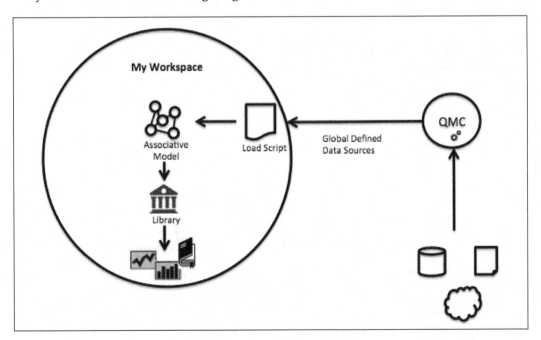

A Qlik Sense application components

Qlik Sense applications are made up of a number of components. Starting from the data source, these components include the following:

- **Global Defined Data Sources** are defined and managed by QMC.

- Based on these governed data sources, a **Load Script** is generated or written, which transforms this data into an **Associative Model**.

- Once the Qlik Sense data model is defined, the developer can determine which fields will have the most value for users in the creation of private sheets for personal analysis. These fields will be used to create dimensions and real-time calculation expressions for measures.

- Additionally, fully defined charts for the most common views of information can be stored in the **Library**.

- Once the Library is defined, sheets (collections of objects), data stories, and bookmarks can be created.

All these components combine to create a dynamic baseline application to be explored by users.

Sharing an application

Let's turn our attention to how an application is shared with the Qlik Sense community.

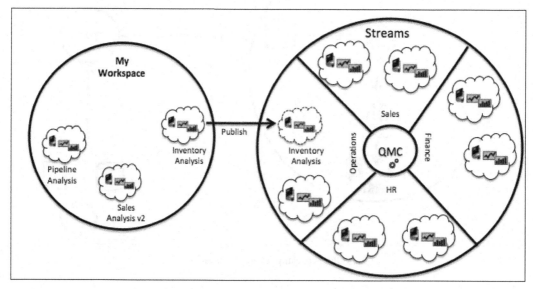

Qlik Sense application publication

Once a Qlik Sense application is complete, the author can share it by publishing it to a stream in the Qlik Sense hub. The publishing process can be accomplished by an administrator who is responsible for a stream and has publishing rights in the QMC. A Qlik Sense developer notifies a stream administrator that a Qlik Sense application is ready for publishing. The stream administrator logs in to the QMC, identifies the Qlik Sense application by name and author, and publishes the application in a stream. This is also the method for applications that are developed on Qlik Sense Desktop.

> This method moves the application from the personal workspace, so a copy of the application should be made prior to publishing. Publishing and best practices for delegating publishing rights to a developer in the QMC will be discussed in more detail in *Chapter 8, Administering Qlik Sense*.

Once an application is published to a stream, it is ready to be explored by users.

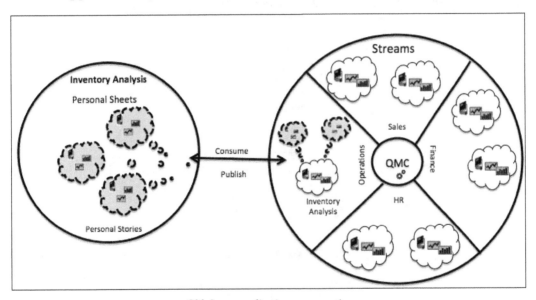

Qlik Sense application consumption

Continuing the application life cycle

One of the key features of a Qlik Sense application is its dynamic nature, which helps meet the broad requirements of data discovery. Users can explore the published sheets and data stories as well as create and share private sheets and stories based on the application library. The library allows for the creation of personal sheets and data stories in a controlled manner. As mentioned earlier, the library is a collection of dimensions, measures, and charts that are defined by the application author and cannot be modified once they are published to a stream. It allows a user to extend an application and share findings through personal sheets and data stories, while keeping consistent definitions across an organization.

Taking a step back, let's look at this new application model. A published Qlik Sense application is just at the beginning of its life cycle. Once published, the application can be expanded by the contributor within the stream using additional published sheets and stories based on the original application.

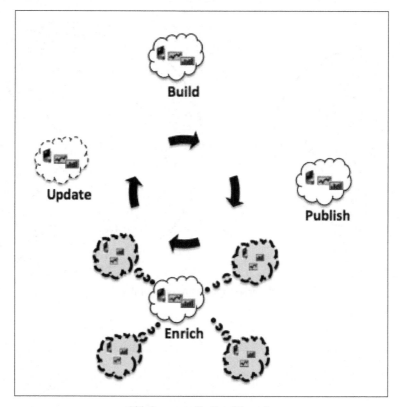

Qlik Sense application life cycle

Summary

A Qlik Sense application is built based on governed data sources defined in the QMC. These data sources are transformed into an associative model. Once the model is defined, key dimensions and measures are created within the library. This library will be used to create sheets. Next, the application is published to a stream within the hub for consumption. The application is then explored by users, and key findings can then be shared through bookmarks, private sheets, and data stories. These artifacts enrich the application and can be published back in the stream for collaboration between other members of the stream.

The next chapter will explore each of these capabilities in more detail and how they meet the needs of key stakeholders within your organization.

5

Empowering Next Generation Data Discovery Consumers

In the previous chapter, we outlined the Qlik® Sense application life cycle, which provided an overview of the key Qlik Sense application components. This chapter's goal is to highlight key features in the context of the specific user requirements that Qlik® has identified as defining a data discovery consumer.

In this chapter, we'll cover the following topics:

- Data discovery consumption requirements
- The hub
- Navigating and leveraging the associative experience

Data discovery consumption requirements

People's expectations of what technology should be and how it should work have been set high with the rise of mobile and touch devices. The notion of a fixed, predictable desktop has changed to a dynamic, unpredictable virtual desktop that exists on whatever device you have access to at the moment. This can include traditional desktop PCs running Windows, laptops, ultrabooks powered by Microsoft Windows, Apple Mac OS, hybrid devices running Windows 8.x, tablets, Chromebooks, smartphones…the list goes on. This new environment requires new approaches in both architecture and application design that create smarter applications to meet the demands of a broader access from varying devices. Qlik Sense was designed from the ground up to meet the diversity of requirements that now exist in your enterprise when it comes to delivering data to support decision-making.

Qlik Sense adapts to very different devices, including a laptop via Microsoft Windows, Apple iPad Air, and finally, an iPhone 5s to name a few. The following screenshot shows the diversity of consumption by users today:

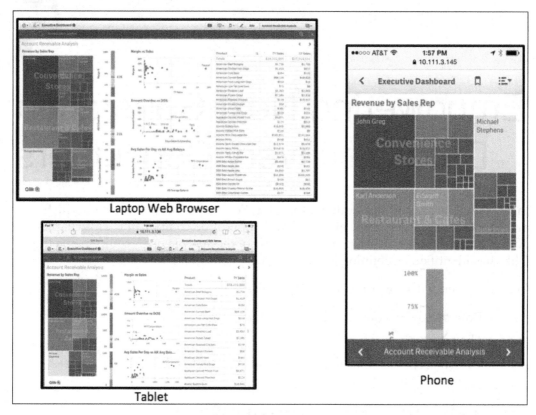

Diversity of consumption

The key thing is that these Qlik Sense screenshots could have been taken using any device on the market. Critically and uniquely, Qlik Sense uses **Responsive Web Design (RWD)** along with progressive disclosure to provide an optimal data discovery experience for users, whatever the form factor of the device. This is at the heart of the Qlik Sense architecture, the aim being for an app to be developed once and consumed/extended across any HTML5-compatible device. For consistency and ease of illustration, the following key components of a Qlik Sense application will be illustrated from a laptop browser, but all these capabilities are available across tablets and smartphones as well. The following key Qlik Sense application components will be reviewed from a consumer perspective where the user has read-only access.

Introducing the hub

As noted in the application life cycle in the previous chapter, Qlik Sense provides a rich collaborative environment that is governed by the QMC through streams. Let's begin our review with the hub, which is the center of a data discovery community. The hub is a collection of streams, which contain Qlik Sense applications. Through the QMC, an administrator defines the streams, and Qlik Sense inherits security access to these streams and applications through security rules. Security rules are covered later in *Chapter 8, Administering Qlik Sense*, and additional detailed examples are available in the Qlik Sense server user guide.

In this case, the consumer, let's call her Nora, has access to a default stream called **Everyone** as well as an administer-defined stream called **BI Center of Excellence**. The hub is designed for touch friendly navigation (that is, it's designed to support selection and navigation using fingers!) between streams on the left-hand side of the display, searching and organizing the view in a number of sorted ways. Let's have a look at the hub:

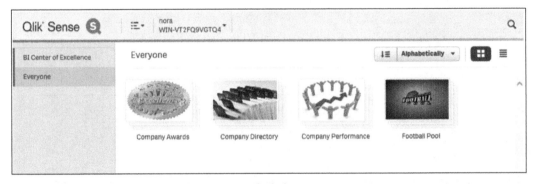

The hub

Now let's turn our attention to streams.

Introducing streams

Streams are an organizing principle for applications as well security. Qlik thinks of streams as work streams for information that can be categorized based on maturity with gradual expansion of access by audience, subject matter, or any other organizing principle. Nora has access to two streams. The **Everyone** stream, which is a public stream created during the server installation, and the **BI Center of Excellence** stream. The **BI Center of Excellence** stream contains a single application called **Executive Dashboard**. **Executive Dashboard** will be used to illustrate how Qlik Sense provides insights to business decision-makers.

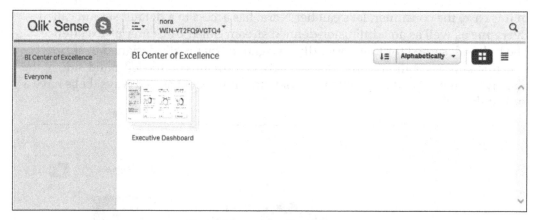

The BI Center of Excellence stream

Let's start with the components of a Qlik Sense application.

Exploring the components of the application

Qlik Sense applications are made up of three main components, which include **Sheets**, **Bookmarks**, and **Stories**. In the case of Nora, who has consumer access, each of these components has been defined by the application developer and is identified by the label **Approved**. This label identifies these items as part of the core components created by the developer and cannot be modified once published.

Sheets

Sheets are a core building block of Qlik Sense. Each sheet contains a collection of objects that are arranged to provide context for analysis on a particular subject. In this case, the sheets are contained in the application called **Executive Dashboard**. Please note that sheets fall into the following three categories:

- **Approved sheets**: These sheets are defined by the author of the application and become read only after publishing. They cannot be modified but can be duplicated as a private sheet for modification.

- **Community sheets**: These sheets are private sheets that have been defined by a user and published to the hub. These can be defined based on duplicated approved sheets and/or new sheets that are assembled through the use of the application library. This will be discussed in detail in the next section, *Realties of data discovery power user*.

- **Private sheets**: These sheets are similar to community sheets but are unpublished so can only be viewed by the author.

In the case of the **Executive Dashboard** application, there are five approved sheets that cover key application areas: **KPI Dashboard**, **Sales Analysis**, **Account Receivables Analysis**, **Inventory Analysis**, and **Product Analysis**. Each of these sheets provides a baseline for the consumer's analysis and exploration.

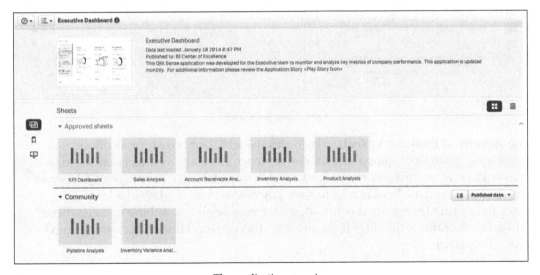

The application overview

Additionally, there are two community sheets, **Pipeline Analysis** and **Inventory Variance Analysis**, which were created by users who have *contributor* access rights. This is a power capability of Qlik Sense that allows users to share key findings across applications. Like community sheets and private sheets, approved sheets are stored with the Qlik Sense application. Please note that since Nora has *consumer* access only, there is no category for her to have personal sheets.

Bookmarks

Qlik Sense continues this popular feature, which was established in QlikView®. Bookmarks allow a user to save the state of a sheet (their selections) so that they can be revisited at a future time, shared, and can be used to create data stories that allow users to combine key discoveries across many Qlik Sense sheets and add additional context through annotations. This example application contains four bookmarks as part of the published application.

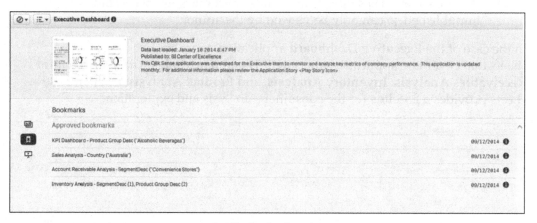

Application bookmarks

The **Approved bookmarks** section includes the KPI dashboard for alcoholic beverages, Australia's sales analysis, convenience store account receivables, and convenience stores' inventory analysis for deli and alcoholic beverages. Qlik Sense consumers can create bookmarks to save key discoveries to view at a later date. Once interesting information is found, a user may wish to combine visualizations and add annotations that highlight any key discoveries. This leads us to our next topic, *Data storytelling*.

Data storytelling

Qlik Sense Stories are a collection of snapshots of key findings (visualization objects) that are assembled to share insights with others in an organization. Snapshots are a graphical representation of the state of visualizations at a certain point in time and are stored in the story media library. Although snapshots are static, they contain embedded bookmarks back in the source sheet, which enables users (or people who want to debate the detail of a narrative) to continue the exploration with live data from the point at which the snapshot was taken. Like Sheets and Bookmarks, approved stories (published with the application by the developer) and community stories (published by users who have contributor rights) can be seen.

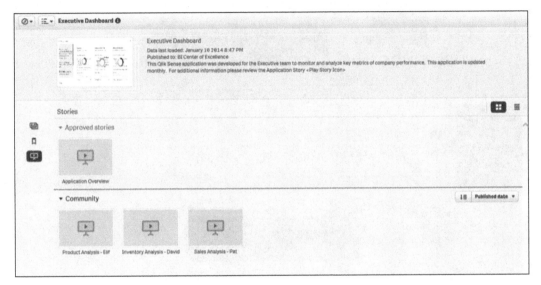

Application stories

The **Executive Dashboard** application, shown in the preceding screenshot, contains four stories available for Nora to review. Community stories were published by Elif, David, and Pat highlighting product analysis, inventory analysis, and sales analysis, respectively. Additionally, there is an approved story named **Application Overview**, which was published as part of the application by the author to outline the goals and use of the application. It is a recommended best practice for application authors to include a story to spur the adoption of an application within the user community. This topic leads us to our next topic, *Navigating and leveraging the associative experience*, in which we will use the **Application Overview** story to provide an overview of the application.

Navigating and leveraging the associative experience

As mentioned earlier, Qlik's intent in building Qlik Sense was to create a user experience that provides a natural and intuitive way to explore data and share key findings. To facilitate our discussion, we will refer to the **Application Overview** story. When selecting an application from the hub, Nora is provided with an application overview. This displays the application name, a short description, and a published date and time that provides key context for the timeliness of the information.

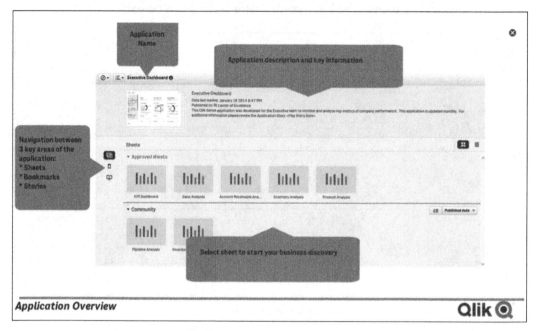

The Executive Dashboard overview

Navigation

Additionally, there are three key areas to explore in a Qlik Sense application; they include sheets (highlighted), bookmarks, and finally, stories, which were discussed earlier. This application contains both approved sheets (developed by the application's author) and community sheets that are the results of contributors who have published private sheets they wish to share with the community. This process will be discussed in detail in the next section.

Now let's open the first sheet named **KPI Dashboard**. As discussed earlier, sheets are an amalgamation of smart objects that display information based on the amount of space available. In **KPI Dashboard**, we can see that the sheet is divided into three key areas: **Expenses**, **Revenue vs Last Year**, and **Accounts Receivables**.

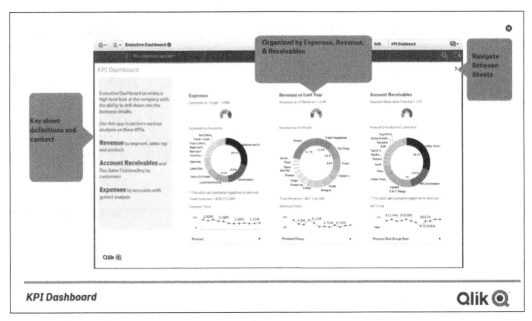

KPI Dashboard

Each of these objects can be used as a filter to see data association and just as importantly, to see nonassociated data (informally known as "The Power of Gray" based on its default coloring that users of QlikView have enjoyed for years). Additionally, each of these objects can be expanded to fullscreen as shown in the next screenshot. The expense spark-line chart can be expanded to fullscreen to reveal additional data points and trends. This also facilitates viewing and selections on mobile devices, where screen real estate is limited.

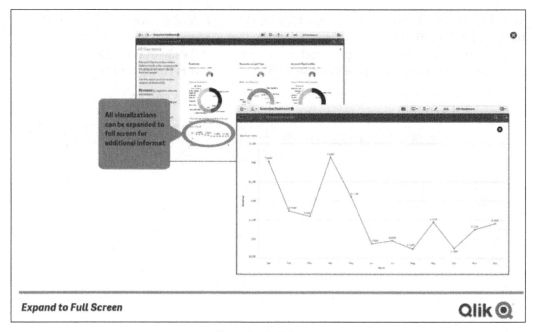

Expand to Full Screen

Smart visualizations

As we review the **Sales Analysis** sheet, there are a number of innovative features that highlight the capabilities of Qlik Sense. First, let's review the sales margin versus sales revenue scatter chart. What makes this chart smart is how Nora interacts with it.

As mentioned earlier, Qlik Sense was developed for mobile devices, which implies touch interaction. In this case, the scatter chart supports multitouch selections on both axes. In this example, Nora has selected to highlight the performance of sales representatives who have margins between 43 percent to 48 percent and sales between 3.68 million to 7 million. Additionally, these selections are in preview mode, which allows Nora to see the impact of these selections before confirming and moving on to the next phase of her discovery.

A second area to highlight is the use of smart scrolling noted in both the **Average Sales Per Day** area and the **Total Revenue by Product Group** horizontal chart. The scroll bars use thumbnails of the chart so that Nora can easily navigate to the key area for review. Additionally, scroll bars appear after the chart has reduced its size to a point where the entire dataset can no longer be shown in the allocated space within the sheet.

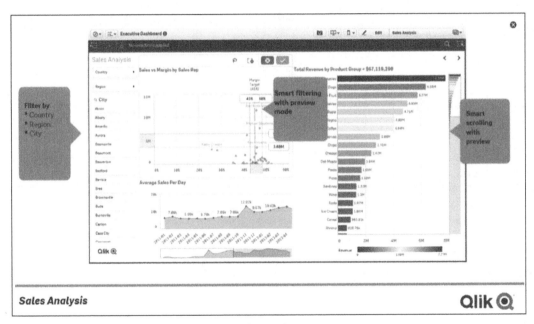

Sales Analysis

Global search

Selections and filtering can also be accomplished through the Qlik Sense global search capabilities. Using the power of the associative engine, Nora can type various products to preview their impact on revenue. In this case, the search was conducted on hot dogs and beer. Note that there is no specific query language needed or requirements to be formed in a specific syntax. Additionally, the result set is shown in preview mode, where the search can be appended and/or modified before commitment to these filters. This facilitates quick interrogation of the data and helps users make more insights.

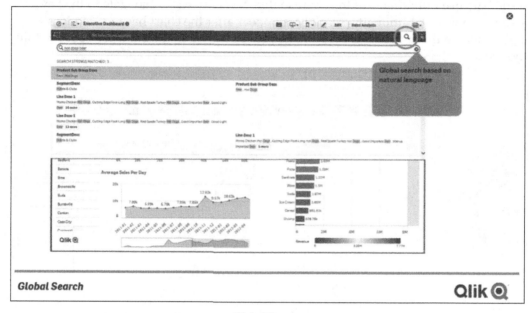

Global Search

Global filtering

To accompany global search, a fully structured approach to filtering is available on every sheet in the top right-hand corner called the global filter. In the global filter, we can see current selections in the top half of the sheet highlighted in green. The bottom half of the sheet is reserved for dimensions that have not been included in the filtering. Please note the associated colors of green for selected elements, white for none selected, and gray for nonassociated elements. Light gray indicates excluded only by selection in the same field, whereas dark gray means excluded by selection in other fields. We can see that the current selections of **ARAge** as **31-60 Days**, **Customers** as **A&R Partners**, and **A2Z Partners** and **AccountDesc** as **Communications** are selected and highlighted in green. If we look at the **Customer** dimension, we see that all other customer names are dark gray because a customer can only have one name in this model. We also see that the other **ARAge** and **AccountDesc** dimension elements are light gray because they are excluded based on selections in other fields. This could change with a change in the selection criteria. Based on this example, global filtering provides a very powerful view of the relationships in the application's associative data model. It also centralizes filtering, leaving valuable screen real estate for visualization based on filtering and the exploration of information.

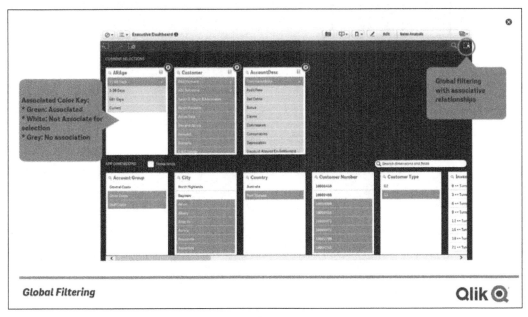

Global Filtering

Now let's turn our attention to the **Account Receivables Analysis** sheet. This sheet is an interesting example of where there are no formal filter panes or listboxes (as there would commonly be in a QlikView app). Instead, each of the objects can be used to select areas to explore, and global filtering and global search can be used to augment or refine the selections at a finer detail level. In this case, revenue contribution for sales representatives by channel is displayed. Qlik Sense also supports a full range of objects, such as the table object to the right, which can be used to filter columns and supports exception formatting for variance reporting.

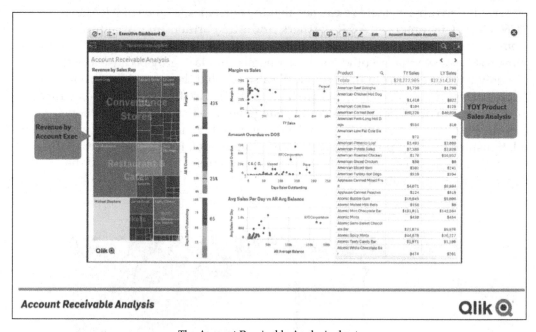

The Account Receivable Analysis sheet

Finally, the table object has the ability to hide and show columns based on the allocated space for the table. The column selection menu within the table allows Nora to orient columns based on the viewable space available to the table.

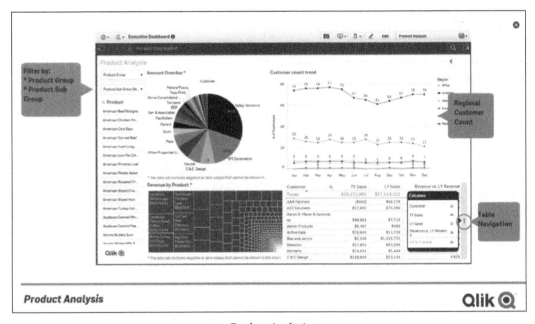

Product Analysis

Extending with Library

As noted in *Chapter 3, The Vision of Qlik Sense*, the rise of BI consumerism and self-service is increasingly becoming an important attribute to meet the needs of the next generation consumers. Qlik Sense embraces this important requirement through **Library**. The Qlik Sense Library is a governed area where an application's author can store dimensions, measures, and preconfigured charts that can be used to create compelling analysis that can be shared across an organization. In this case, Nora is taking advantage of the **Trended Revenue over time** line chart to create or extend an application.

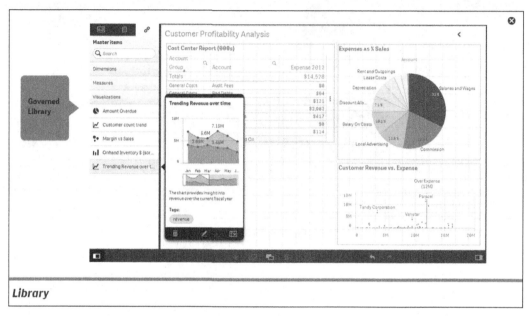

Qlik Sense Library

The Qlik Sense Library is at the center of a broad range of governed self-service capabilities that drives insight within an organization.

Summary

In summary, this chapter covered how Qlik Sense meets the new requirements of consuming and extending discovery-based applications, meeting these requirements across a myriad of platforms spanning PC, Mac, and the never-ending flow of new mobile devices. This required Qlik Sense to be built with a new approach that is responsive to these new realities of self-service and mobile use. Now let's turn our attention to the contributor who seeks to not only consume but also extend and share their data discovery insights.

6
Contributing to Data Discovery

In the previous chapter, we outlined data discovery consumption requirements, which provided an overview of key Qlik® Sense capabilities for users who wish to consume an application that is prebuilt. This chapter's goal is to highlight key features in the context of the specific user requirements that Qlik® has identified as being needed by a data discovery contributor, or someone who seeks to share key findings from their analysis.

In this chapter, we will cover the following topics of Qlik Sense:

- Data discovery contributor requirements
- Bookmarks
- Private sheets
- Private stories
- Publishing to an existing application

Realities of the data discovery contributor

One of the strengths of Qlik Sense applications is the ability to share and extend the value of applications with other members of the stream. As noted in *Chapter 4, Overview of a Qlik Sense Application's Life Cycle*, there are number of useful ways to share key business discoveries. These include the following:

- Bookmarks
- Private sheets
- Stories

Each of these capabilities help analysts not only consume Qlik Sense applications but also share and spur additional conversation and insights. The stream administrator covered in the *Chapter 8, Administering Qlik Sense*, enables these contributor capabilities. Let's take a closer look at each of these capabilities through the role of an analyst named Pat.

Creating private bookmarks

A private bookmark is the beginning of an analysis that drives collaboration across an organization. Bookmarks allow a developer and contributor to save the state of a sheet within a Qlik Sense application. In the previous example, the **Executive Dashboard** application, the author defined approved bookmarks. These public bookmarks are part of the published application to help users start their data discovery process. This capability is also available to contributors to save key business discoveries for a later time.

For example, say Pat conducts a sales analysis on products sold in key cities, as shown in the city's sales analysis in the following screenshot:

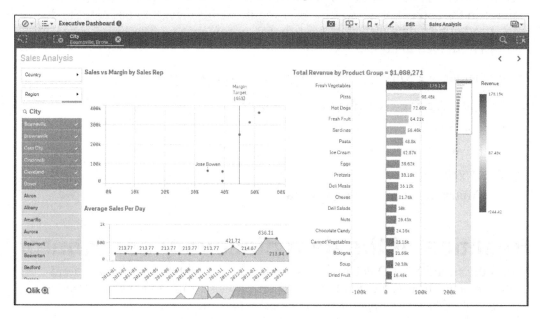

Pat has selected six key cities for analysis of sales rep resentative performance and products sold. This view is interesting so Pat decides to bookmark this sheet with these selections. Note that when selecting the bookmark icon, all approved and saved private bookmarks are available for navigation. Additionally, the **Create new bookmark** button is available and will automatically create a default title based on the sheet name and selections:

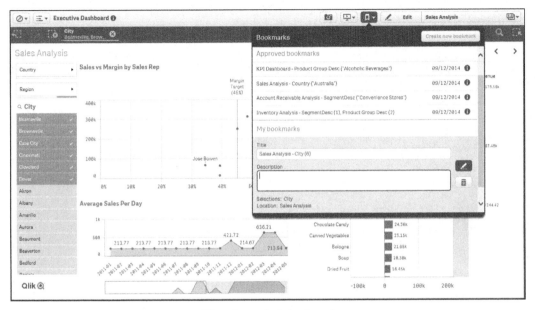

City sales analysis bookmark

Once saved, the bookmark becomes a part of the application under **My bookmarks** and can only be accessed by the creator, which in this case is Pat.

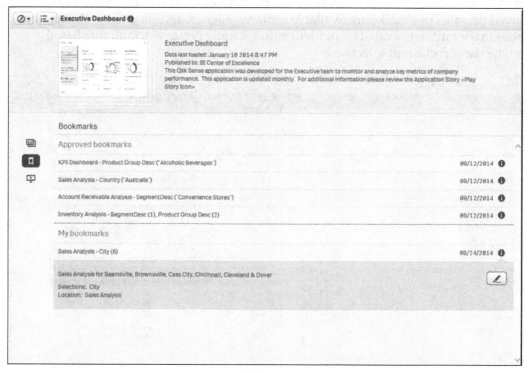

Executive Dashboard bookmark

To summarize, simple Qlik Sense Bookmarks can play an important part in bringing context to the beginning of an analysis as well as saving key insights gained from an analysis. Although separate features, Qlik is seeing early adopters use Bookmarks as the start of building critical mass with insight that can be shared through published sheets and stories, which are the topics of our next sections.

Creating and sharing private sheets

As discussed in *Chapter 4*, *Overview of a Qlik Sense Application's Life Cycle*, the building block of a Qlik Sense application is a sheet. In the **Executive Dashboard** community, we can see the sheets associated with the **Executive Dashboard** application. These include **Approved sheets** (published by the application author), **My sheets**, which are private sheets defined by the contributor (Pat), and finally, **Community**, which are private sheets published by other contributors.

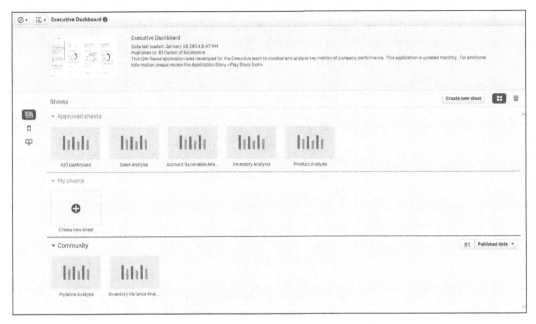

Executive Dashboard community

Let's now dig a bit deeper into how these sheets are built. There are two main ways in which private sheets are built, as follows:

- Duplicate an approved sheet
- Create a new sheet

In both cases, a key feature that allows a contributor to build strongly governed private sheets is the Qlik Sense Library. The Qlik Sense Library is a key component of an application that allows the author to expose key portions of the associative model in the form of **Dimensions**, **Measures**, **Charts**, and predefined **Visualizations**. How the Qlik Sense Library is created will be covered in more detail in the next chapter. The following screenshot shows **Library**:

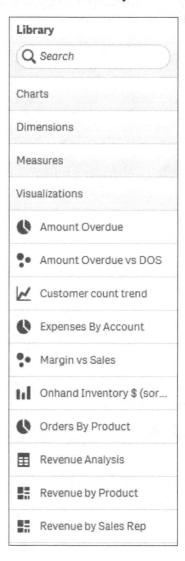

Creating a private sheet

Let's now turn our attention to creating a private sheet by the first method, duplicating an existing sheet, and then editing it to meet your requirements. The advantage of this method is that Pat can start the creation of her product analysis based on the approved **Product Analysis** sheet. The process begins with selecting the sheet that best aligns with the content you wish to analyze. In this case, Pat wishes to create a product analysis that integrates the inventory on hand with the approved **Product Analysis** sheet. As the **Product Analysis** sheet is an approved sheet, it cannot be edited and must first be duplicated before changes can be made.

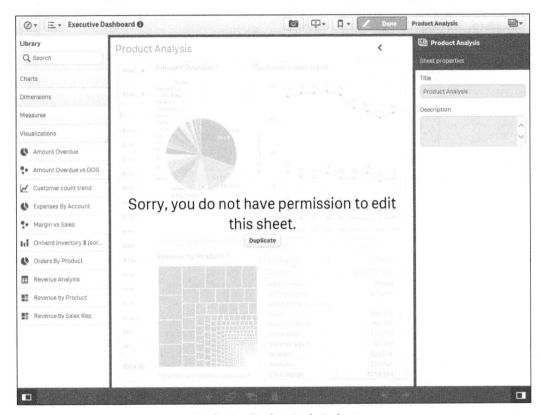

Duplicating Product Analysis sheet

Once the sheet is duplicated, it is automatically converted into a private sheet, where Pat can rename and alter the content and layout of the sheet through the use of **Library**. Please note that Pat has renamed the sheet to `Pat-Product Analysis` as well as added a helpful description, which highlights the goals of this sheet, which is `This analysis highlights both Revenue by Product and the ability to fulfill the orders (On hand Inventory$) to recognize revenue.` Additionally, there is a wide selection of preconfigured charts as well as dimensions and measures she can take advantage of in **Library**. In this example, Pat will replace the customer count line chart with the **Onhand Inventory $ (sorted by Sales Qty)** horizontal bar chart from **Library**. This is one example of a variety of governed changes available to Pat in designing a new sheet. We will explore the breadth of changes to develop private sheets in the next section.

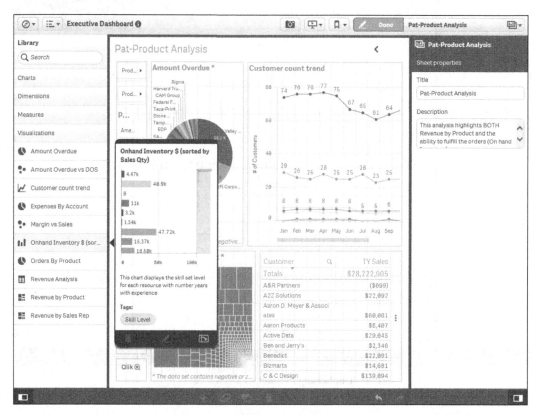

Creating the Pat-Product Analysis sheet

With the **Onhand Inventory $ (sorted by Sales Qty)** chart from **Library** dragged and dropped onto the sheet, Pat is ready to end the editing process. Since this process is all server-based, there is no need to save the sheet but rather just click on the **Done** button.

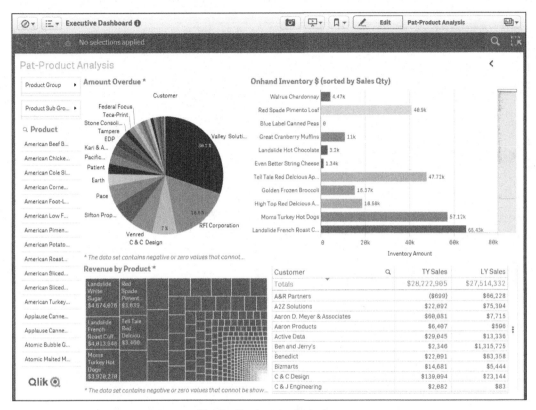

The Pat-Product Analysis sheet

Publishing a private sheet

Now that the sheet is complete, let's return to the application overview. As you can see in the following screenshot, **My sheets** now contains a new sheet called **Pat-Product Analysis**, and with a right-click, it is ready to be published to the community:

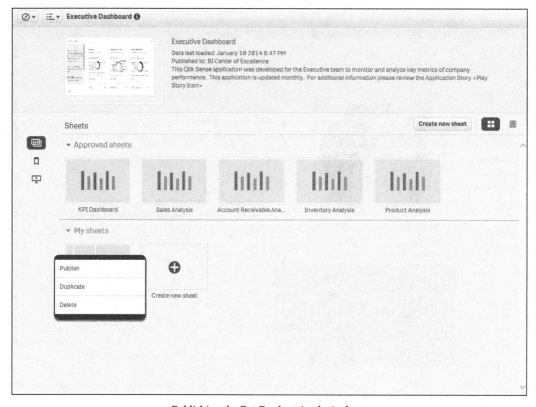

Publishing the Pat-Product Analysis sheet

When the sheet is published, a new section will appear called **Published by me** that contains all published sheets by Pat. Also, note that Pat has a number of sheets that are in progress in the **My sheets** section.

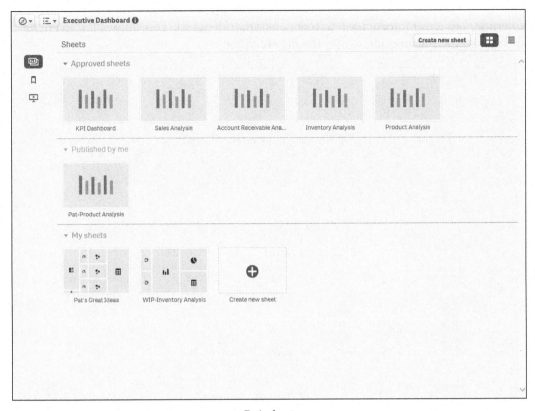

Pat's sheets

In summary, a duplicated approved sheet is an excellent way to start the creation of a private sheet as it has the advantage of leveraging the existing defined sheets from the published application or the work of other analysts in the community. Now let's turn our attention to creating a new sheet.

Creating a new sheet

A second approach to sharing key business insights is to create a new sheet. As shown in **Creating a New Sheet** in the following screenshot, Pat creates a new sheet called `Revenue Pipeline Analysis`, which contains both order information and inventory on–hand information to meet customer demand. This allows Pat to create and share new information across the organization.

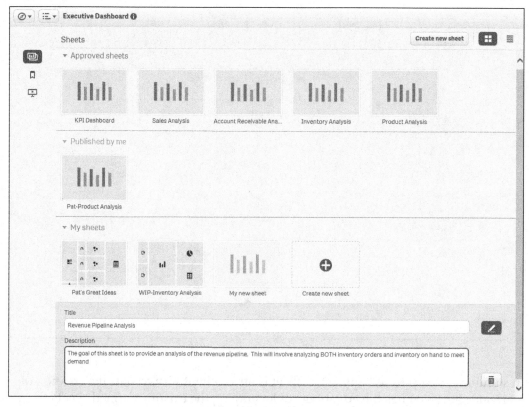

Creating a new sheet

Once the sheet is created, **Library** and sheet properties are exposed and the sheet appears with a faint grid. This grid is a part of the responsive web design experience and facilitates the orientation and placement of objects from **Library**. This not only helps in the creation of the sheet but also plays a key role in how the objects will be viewed and consumed across multiple devices. Also, note that the creation and assembly of new objects is easily done by users due to the associative engine. Because of the associative model, every object is connected and no developer prewiring is required. The associative engine permeates the use of Qlik Sense, not only its use, but also the creation of compelling solutions.

Adding a predefined visualization to a new sheet

One of the key areas Pat is interested in is the customer revenue this year and in the previous year to help her better anticipate customer demand. Hopefully, the author of the application anticipated this common request and stored a table chart under **Visualizations** in **Library**. Specifically, the **Revenue Analysis** table chart is available in **Library** with a thumbnail shown to help Pat evaluate its applicability to the sheet content.

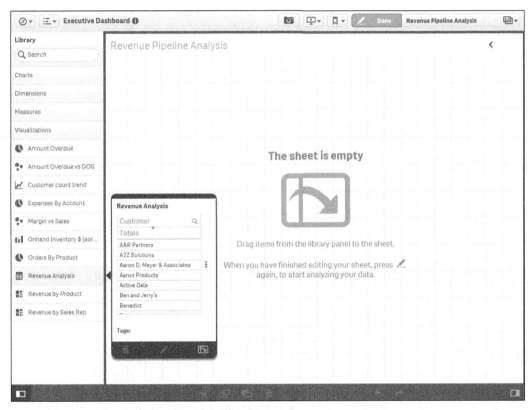

Adding a predefined visualization to a new sheet

Adding the **Revenue Analysis** object is a simple drag and drop movement. Please note that the sheet grid will automatically make recommendations on the placement of the object.

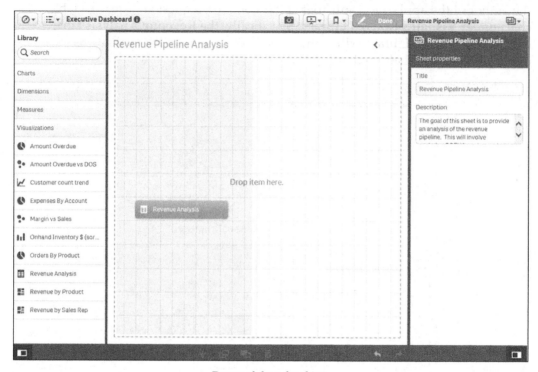

Drag and drop the object

Creating a Combo chart object

Once the object is placed, Pat notices that there are no visualizations available that allow her to see the trend of inventory on hand and sales orders. This requires her to create a new chart based on dimensions and measures defined in **Library**. So to begin this process, Pat selects and drags **Combo chart** to the sheet noted in the following screenshot:

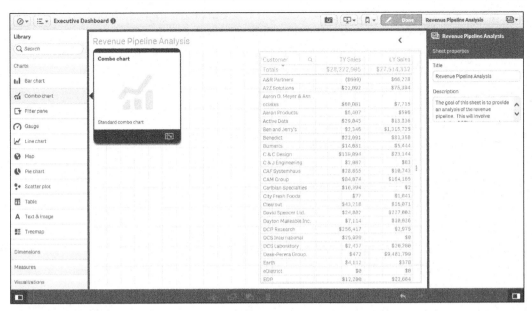

Creating a Combo chart object

Once the Combo chart is in position, the object guides Pat on the requirements for visualization. The object highlights the requirement of at least one dimension and a measure. To speed the task, the Qlik Sense search capability can be used to find the dimension; in this case, **Year Month**.

Adding a dimension

The next step is to add the measures; as this is **Combo chart**, there will be two measures. The first measure added will be **Sales Quantity**. **Sales Quantity** is available in **Measures** and a tooltip reveals the expression, which defines how it is defined.

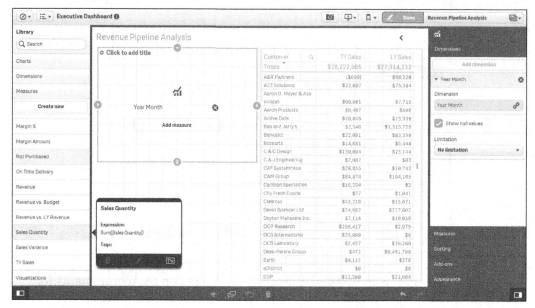

Adding a Sales Quantity measure

Additionally, as the measures are dragged and dropped on **Combo chart**, the object continues to guide Pat on how to visualize the data. Qlik Sense provides guidance to add the inventory quantity and options for display. **Combo chart** supports bar, line, and marker chart types. In this case, Pat selects a line to compliment the **Sales Quantity** measure that is already displayed as a bar.

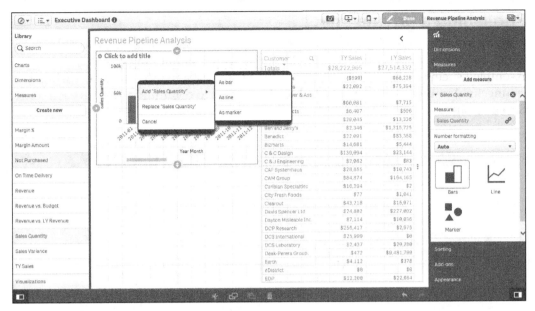

Adding the Inventory Quantity measure

Finally, Pat completes the sheet layout by adding the **Onhand Inventory $ (sorted by Sales Qty)** chart available in the **Visualizations** portion of **Library**, shown as follows:

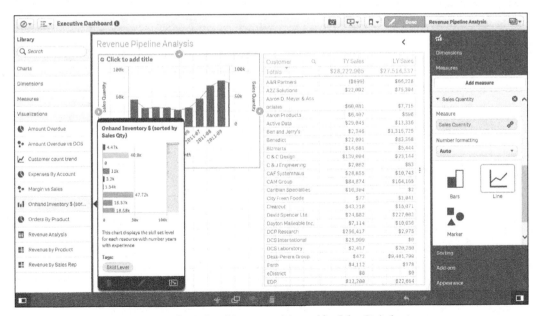

Adding the Onhand Inventory $ (sorted by Sales Qty) chart

Publishing a private sheet

With the new **Revenue Pipeline Analysis** sheet completed, Pat is ready to publish with a right-click as described earlier. Also, it is worth mentioning that this assembled sheet is fully selectable during the process of assembly, and no wiring (connecting) of these objects is needed to allow them to communicate with each other across all sheets.

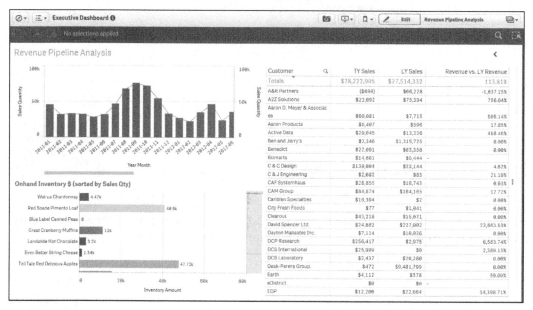

Completed Revenue Pipeline Analysis sheet

Once the sheet is published, it is available to the **Executive Dashboard** application, where it can be consumed, duplicated, and expanded by other members of the community.

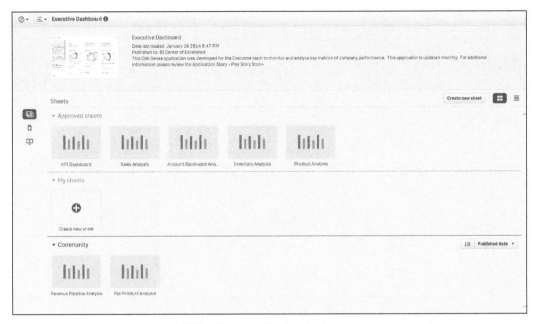

Published Revenue Pipeline Analysis sheet

In summary, creating new sheets provides an alternative way to collaborate with members of the application's community. It allows contributors in a governed environment to start with a blank sheet to organize and share their thoughts and insights, and is managed centrally in the Qlik Management Console. Now let's turn our attention to creating a Qlik Sense story, which adds additional capabilities for collaboration.

Creating and sharing stories

Qlik Sense Stories provide an additional capability to collaborate and share business discoveries within the Executive Dashboard community. In the story overview, we can see that similar to Bookmarks and Sheets, Stories have **Approved stories** (defined by the author of the application), **My stories** (private and only viewable by the author), and **Community** (published) sections. We covered the role of approved stories as a way for application authors to provide an overview about the application and intended use.

In this section, we will focus on the creation of a story by a contributor (Pat) who will use this capability to present a sales analysis to the community.

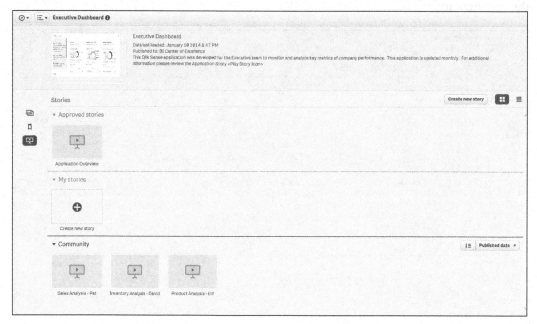

Story overview

Defining a story

To begin with, Pat creates a new story by selecting the **Create new story** option under **My stories**. The default name is **My new story**, which Pat changes to Sales Analysis - Pat to reflect the goal of the story. Additionally, a description can be added to provide information on the goals of the story.

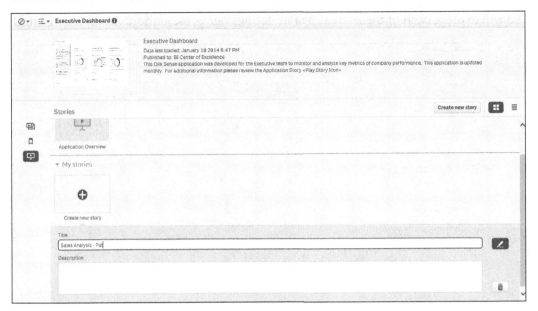

Defining a story

Once the story is defined, Pat enters the story workspace, which provides a broad set of tools to create rich presentations that are dynamically linked to the Qlik Sense application. The story workspace contains the ability to create sheets as well as access the following libraries:

- Snapshot
- Text
- Shape
- Effect
- Media

We will explore each of these areas as Pat defines her presentation.

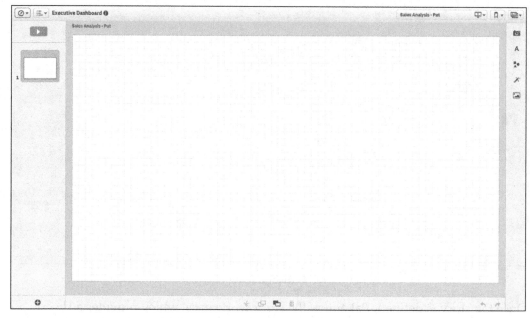

Story workspace

Creating snapshots

Let's start with creating snapshots. The ability to create a snapshot is a general capability found on all sheets within an application. By selecting the camera, all objects for which snapshots can be created are highlighted with an orange outline. Additionally, each object also contains an indicator that highlights the number of times snapshots have been created for the object. As you can see, Pat has been quite busy in selecting key objects for her story.

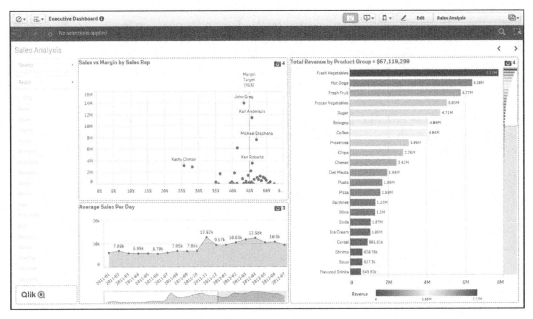

Creating snapshots

Now that Pat has selected her snapshots, she prepares to organize them in a story. Note that all snapshots are stored in **Snapshot Library**.

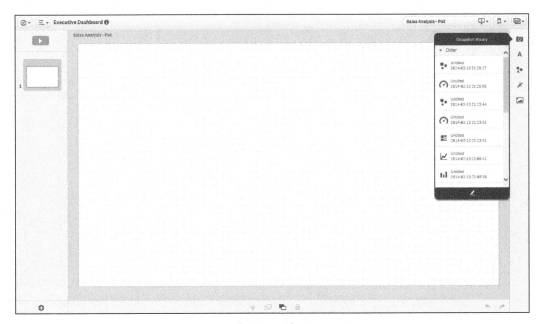

Story snapshots

These snapshots are organized by the date and time when they were taken. This is an important consideration because it means that snapshots are like photos, storing the visualization and data of the time the snapshot was taken. By design, snapshots are not updated when the application data is changed.

Once the snapshots are taken, Pat locates the shot and then drags and drops it onto the grid. Also, note that each snapshot can be edited with the ability to modify some of the properties that can include turning on/off titles and labels.

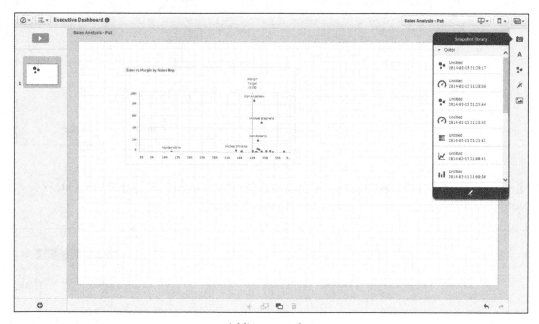

Adding a snapshot

Adding text

Now let's add text to this sheet, which is accomplished through **Text library**. **Text library** facilitates both the creation of titles as well as paragraphs that can be used to add comments to highlight key business discoveries.

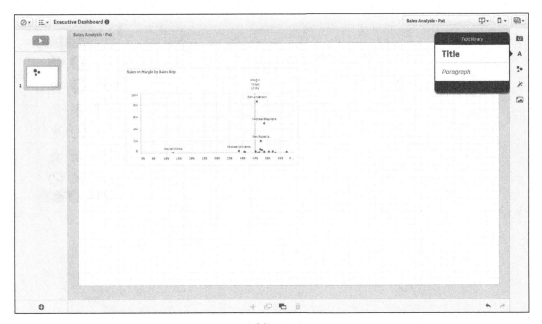

Adding text

Adding shapes

Pat has added the title **High Margin Sales** and emphasized it with bold and underline styles. Additionally, there is **Shape library**, which allows the integration of various shapes to highlight and emphasize the story.

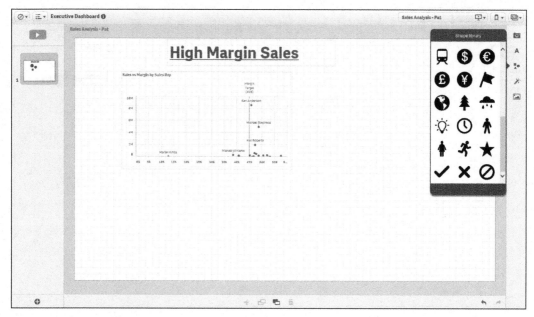

Adding a shape

Pat chose the light bulb symbol to identify key ideas in this story. The symbol's default color is black, but can be changed. Additionally, there is **Effect library**, which can be used to highlight the lowest, highest, or a particular value within a chart.

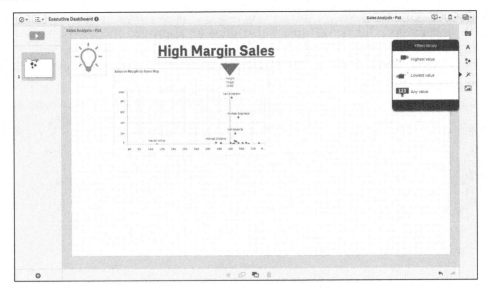

Adding effects

Media library

The final major area is **Media library**, which allows contributors the ability to add images from outside Qlik Sense. Images are made available and managed by the Qlik Management Console through **Content library**. Additional information on this process is available in *Chapter 8, Administering Qlik Sense*.

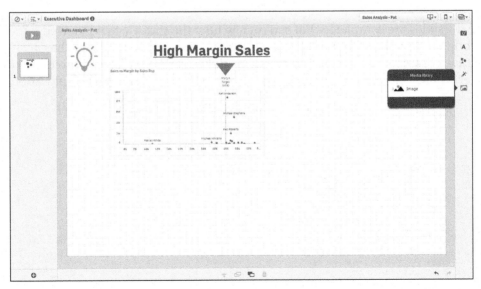

Adding media

Additionally, Pat would like to add a portion of the **Sales Analysis** application directly in her story. Qlik Sense Stories also allow an approved sheet to be embedded within the **Sales Analysis** story. This enables Pat to share her analysis through a number of slides and also allows the viewer the ability to continue their exploration through an active sheet.

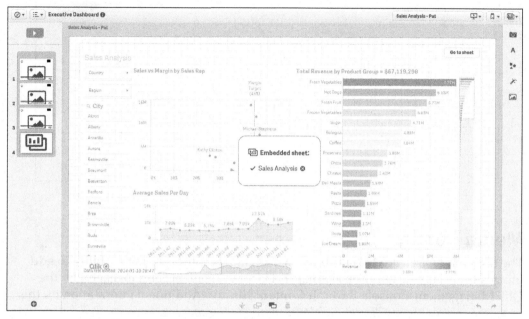

Adding a dynamic slide

Once the slides are completed, Pat can review how the slides will be viewed by selecting the Play the story button. Also, note that each of the snapshots has an embedded bookmark that can be selected by right-clicking on **View source**, and the viewer will be directed back to the application sheet to continue their exploration.

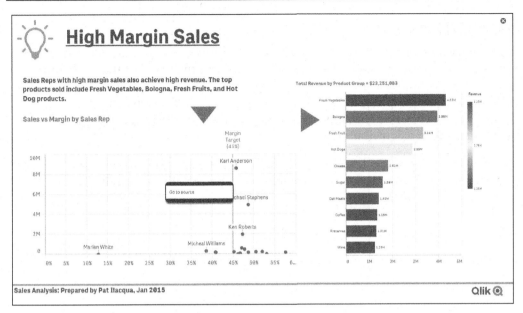

Final review

Publishing your story

Now that Pat is comfortable with the **Sales Analysis** story, the publishing process is similar to the publishing process of private sheets. To accomplish this, as illustrated, Pat right-clicks and selects **Publish** to move the story to the community and make it read only.

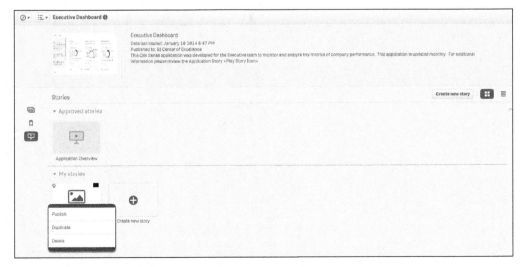

Publishing the story

Summary

In summary, one of the strengths of Qlik Sense applications is the ability it offers to contributors to actively share, collaborate, and extend the value of the application with members of the stream. Qlik Sense has a number of exciting ways to share key business discoveries. These include bookmarks, published sheets, and stories. Each of these approaches is highly governed and provides a wide range of capabilities to meet the needs of a contributor.

In the next chapter of this book, we will explore using the skills we learned alongside some ideas of best practices in how to create author-engaging applications for Qlik Sense.

7
Creating Engaging Applications

In the previous chapters, we looked at the application life cycle and the different roles of users: the consumer and the contributor. Having established the basic requirements, in this chapter we will dive into the details of app creation and discuss how it is done. We'll also look at best practices of visualization and how to employ them using Qlik Sense.

In this chapter, we will discuss the following topics:

- The process of building an app
- Data connectors
- The data model viewer
- Sheet objects—Visualizations
- Best practices
- Migrating QlikView applications into Qlik Sense

Preparations and requirements

Often the initial step in building an app is that you have some data that you want to analyze, but you don't necessarily know exactly what you want to look for in the data. As a business user, you can—and should—just load this data into Qlik Sense and start developing. Our experience is that the best way to develop the app is to start *without* first defining the requirements.

The reason is that when you load data and start to create visualizations, you *learn* from data. This knowledge is very important once you start defining what you want to analyze. Hence, you should first develop a basic app, then take a break and evaluate what you learned. *Now* is the right time to start formulating the requirements.

Another common case is the opposite situation: you know that you want to calculate a specific KPI, for example, supplier efficiency, but you don't necessarily know what data you need to be able to do this. In this case, you need to start with some research about where to find the relevant information, that is, in which database and which tables.

The requirement specifications

If you define a larger project, you will use what you know as a starting point for the requirement specifications for your app. The following questions might pop up:

- **Data**: Which data sources should be used? Which tables should be used? How should the tables be linked? Are there common keys? Is there more than one source for the transactions? Are there tables missing? How should the customer hierarchy be resolved?

- **KPIs**: Which calculations should be made: turnover, profit, cost, delivery accuracy, or product quality? Which definition of gross margin should be used? How should the given discount affect the calculation of a salesman's bonus? Which accumulations are needed: year-to-date or month-to-date?

- **Dimensions**: How should the KPIs be displayed: per year, per customer, per salesman, per region, or per product? Which comparisons should be made: year-over-year or month-over-month? Are there drill-down hierarchies that need to be defined?

- **Security**: Is the data confidential? Who gets to see what? Can we allow offline usage? Is the authorization data-driven or static? Do we need to include authorization information in the data model, or can we postpone the decision around security?

You will soon realize that creating the requirement specification is not an easy task.

Discovery of requirements

Discovering exactly what users, stakeholders, and sponsors want you to create is often the most difficult part of a business intelligence project. The communication between IT experts and nontechnical business users is often full of misunderstandings and misinterpretations. Business users often don't know what they want until they see it, and they frequently can't articulate their expectations in languages that IT experts use to design systems.

Few business users will know what **data model** really means, so expecting them to be able to exactly define the requirements in technical terms is futile. Experienced authors can extract this information through discussions and clever questioning, but the number of people who are able to do this within an organization is limited.

IT professionals often frame their requirement questions in technical language, for example, "Which table in the database should be used?" or "Which fields should be used to calculate the KPI?". However, business users may not have the technical knowledge to respond to these questions. Business users often explain their expectations in a technically vague language, which is not specific enough for designers to develop solutions.

On the other hand, *the business user is the customer*. The very reason why we develop an app in the first place is to supply the business user with a tool to analyze and learn from data. So, the requirement specifications *must* focus on the business user.

Step-wise implementation

The solution to the problem of business users understanding technical language is to use a step-wise implementation where the app developer iteratively finds the requirements, develops the app further, tests what has been done, and finally evaluates the app together with the business user. The evaluation will lead to new requirements and to changes or refinements of the old requirements. The steps must be small and the typical cycle is hours or days.

In other words, you *discover* the requirements together with the business user. As the development proceeds, the app will converge to the needs of the business user.

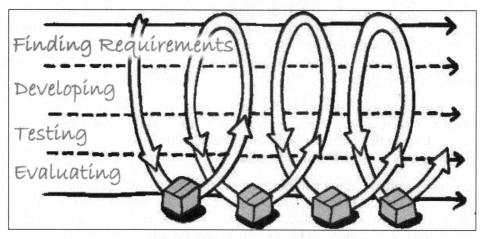

The iterative development process

This means that you *cannot* begin your app development with a detailed requirement specification. Rather, you should start with a very basic specification containing information about some of the needed data sources and ideas of some of the wanted visualizations.

Hence, irrespective of whether you are a business user or an app developer responsible for data modeling and difficult formulas, you should start by spending an hour or so to load the data and create some graphs with the goal to *learn* from data. Then, you are in a much better position to define or discuss requirements further.

The process

The first step in building the app is to load the data. The data can be one single table or several tables linked logically by **key fields**. Key fields are fields that exist in more than one table and link rows in one table with rows in another. Together, they form a data model.

When you have a data model, you can start building the layout, which consists of different objects, for example, lists, graphs, tables, and filter panes, placed on different worksheets. The objects can contain formulas that define different calculations that will be calculated as the user makes their selections.

The model explained previously assumes that you have both a developer and a business user that participate in the development process. In real life, you will notice that the initial development efforts will be like this, but as the app takes shape, the business users will want to do more and more on their own—which is good. After all, the goal is to have business users who are self-sufficient and create apps as much as possible on their own.

Getting started with the app creation

When you first open Qlik Sense, you come to the hub. This is the place where you have an overview of all your apps. The hubs look slightly different in the Desktop and server versions, but they are essentially the same. The following screenshot shows what a hub looks like:

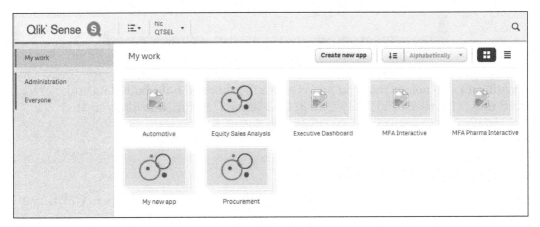

The Qlik Sense hub

Creating a new app

In Qlik Sense Desktop, you are greeted with a dialog where you are asked to create an app as shown in the following screenshot. In Qlik Sense server, you will find the corresponding functionality on a button on the right-hand side in the toolbar.

The Qlik Sense Desktop welcome dialog

Creating an app means that you will create a file that will hold both data and everything else needed to analyze it. In Qlik Sense Desktop, this file is created in `C:\Users\hic\Documents\Qlik\Sense\Apps`.

Loading your data

Once you have named and opened your app, you will get a screen where Qlik Sense asks you to load your data.

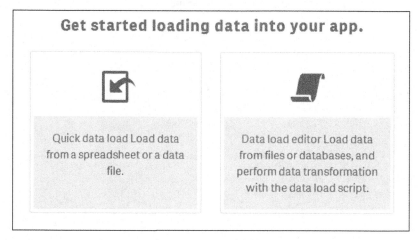

The getting started dialog

When you have this option before you, you can load data in several different ways. The easiest way is to drag and drop a spreadsheet or a file onto Qlik Sense, or to click on the **Quick data load** command and select the file in a file browser, as shown in the following screenshot:

Dropping a file onto an app

This will open a file wizard where you can tweak the details of how the file should be loaded so that you get the data you want, as shown in the following screenshot:

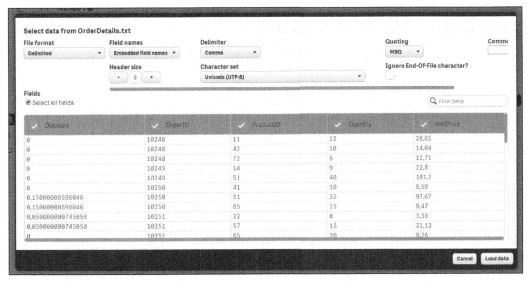

The file wizard

You can specify file type, whether the file contains empty lines at the top (before the data starts), whether the first line contains the field names or not, and so on. Make sure you get all the settings right before you click on **Load data**.

Clicking on **Load data** will store your settings and load the data; if everything goes well, you will get the following dialog:

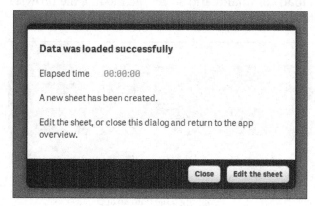

Data was loaded successfully

Elapsed time   00:00:00

A new sheet has been created.

Edit the sheet, or close this dialog and return to the app overview.

Close   Edit the sheet

The success message, which is shown once data is loaded

At this stage, you can either start to edit the sheet or you can load additional tables.

Loading additional tables

It is very common that the data you want to analyze is stored in several different tables, for example:

- One table for the orders (one row per order)
- One table for the customers who placed the orders (one row per customer)
- One table for the order lines (one row per order line)
- One table for the products (one row per product)

In a normal database, there are rules about where different entities are stored. For instance, everything about the customers should be stored in the Customers table. If you need some information about a customer in another table, a unique customer identifier is stored in this table, which means that all the necessary data can be retrieved by a simple lookup in the Customers table.

For the previously discussed case, the Order Lines table will contain both the order ID and the product ID, and the Orders table will contain the customer ID. This way, all four tables are linked logically, as shown in the following screenshot:

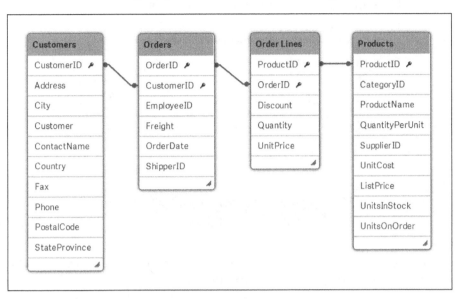

A simple data model made from four tables

To obtain this data model in your app, you need to repeat the procedure for loading data that we had discussed previously for each additional table. You can either drag and drop a file onto Qlik Sense, or you can use the **Quick data load** command in the toolbar menu.

In the **Quick data load** process, you need to make sure that the key fields are named the same in all tables and that no other fields have the same name.

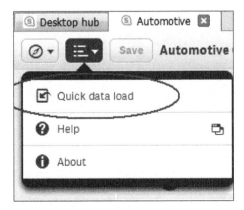

The Quick data load command

Either way, you will get a dialog asking you whether you want to add or replace data. You almost always want to add data. In this context, **Replace data** means that you remove all previously loaded data and replace it with the table you are about to load. These options are shown in the following screenshot:

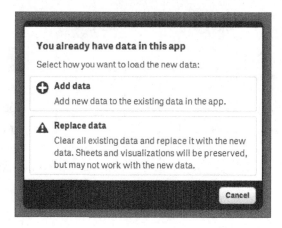

This will take you to the familiar file wizard shown in the previous section, where you can define the file properties of the additional table.

Using Data load editor

On the screen where Qlik Sense asked you to load your data, there was a second option: **Data load editor**. Clicking on this option will open a new tab with a script editor, as shown in the following screenshot:

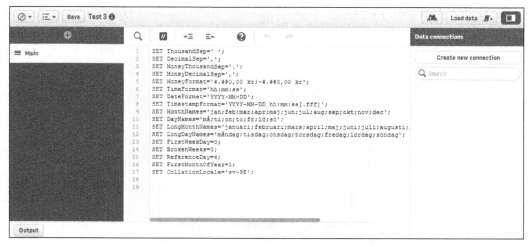

The Qlik Sense Data load editor

This editor is very similar to the QlikView script editor. It allows you to make very complex data transformations and basically load anything. However, as with all powerful tools, it is also easy to make mistakes. Use it with caution.

When you define your data using drag and drop or the **Quick data load** command, the data load sequence will be stored in the load script as one or several Load statements. This means that these can be edited in **Data load editor** if you want to tweak them after they have been created.

You can also create your script from scratch using **Data load editor**. If so, you must first create your data connections. These can be file folders, connections to regular databases, or connections to other data sources using other connectors. This is how you do it:

1. Open **Data load editor** from the initial dialog of the menu in the toolbar.

The Data load editor command

 Clicking on the icon to the right in the menu will open **Data load editor** in a new tab.

2. Now you will have **Data load editor** open. To the right, you have the **Data connections** panel. If you click on the **Create new connection** button, you will open a menu where you can choose the connection type and then specify the properties of the connection in the following dialog:

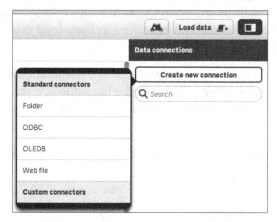

Adding a data connection

Creating a database connection

If you want to create a database connection using **Open Database Connectivity (ODBC)**, you should choose **ODBC**. This opens the ODBC connection dialog, where you can choose which data source to use:

The ODBC connections dialog

The data sources that you see are the ones defined in the Windows operating system, which means that if you do the development on a server, the list is limited to those defined by the server administrator.

Once you have created these connections, you will have them displayed in a list of data connections, as shown in the following screenshot:

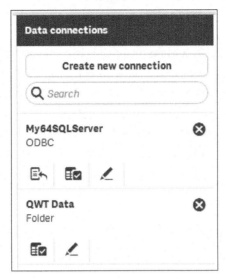

The list of data connections

Each data connection has several icons: an icon to create a Load or a Select statement and a second one to edit the connection itself. In addition, database connections have a third icon that is used to create a Connect statement.

Hence, to create a Load statement, you should click on and find the file that contains the table. This way, you can create a script in very much the same way as you would in QlikView if you are familiar with it.

The goal is to create a script that defines a logical, coherent data model that corresponds to the business situation. When you have created the script, you need to run it to load the data. This is done by clicking on the **Load data** button in the toolbar of **Data load editor**.

Associative model assumptions

In principle, each Load or Select statement creates one table in the data model. There are, however, some exceptions to this rule:

- If a loaded table contains exactly the same set of fields as an existing data table, the new table will not be created as a separate table. Instead, it will be appended to the existing table.

- If the Load or Select statement is preceded by the Concatenate keyword or Join, the loaded table will be merged with an existing data table.

- If the Load or Select statement is preceded by the Generic keyword, the loaded table will be transformed into several data tables.

- If the Load or Select statement is preceded by the Mapping or Semantic keyword, the loaded table will not be used as a normal data table.

- An existing table can be deleted using the Drop command.

Several Load statements will thus normally create a data model with several tables.

In the end of the script run, the existing tables will be evaluated. If the same field name is found in more than one table, this field will be considered to be a key that links the two tables. This way, a data model is created. The logic in the script evaluation is hence identical in Qlik Sense and QlikView.

The data model – the core of the logic

The data model defines how Qlik Sense's internal logical inference and calculations should be made.

A user selection implies a new logical situation. Other field values than the ones used before are possible; summations need to be made, so the charts and the KPIs get different values than what we got before. Everything needs to be recalculated, and the data model defines how this is done.

When the user makes a selection, Qlik Sense first evaluates which field values of other fields are possible and which records are possible. In this evaluation, the key fields are used to propagate the selection to other tables. The second step is to calculate all formulas based on the possible records. The data model thus defines *how* all calculations should be made.

When you create your data model, you should look out for two potential problems: synthetic keys and circular references. Synthetic keys are simply Qlik Sense's way of managing composite keys. Usually, you do not want synthetic keys—you want one single key in each table link. However, if you know that you have multiple keys linking two tables, and that is the way you want your data model, then there is no problem in having synthetic keys.

This is not the case for circular references. If you have a circular reference, you should rethink your data model with the goal of removing the loop. Qlik Sense will, at the end of the script run, warn you about these potential problems, as shown in the following screenshot:

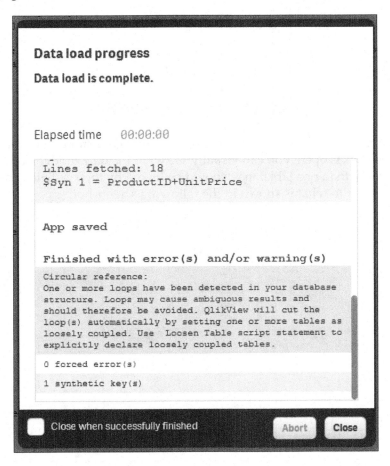

Using Data model viewer

The script defines the data model, but if you want to view it graphically, you should use **Data model viewer**. This is opened from the toolbar menu, as shown in the following screenshot:

Clicking on the icon to the right in the menu will open **Data model viewer** in a new tab. Once this is open, you can visually see what the data model looks like. If you have more than one table, they should be linked by the key fields and look something similar to what is shown in the following screenshot:

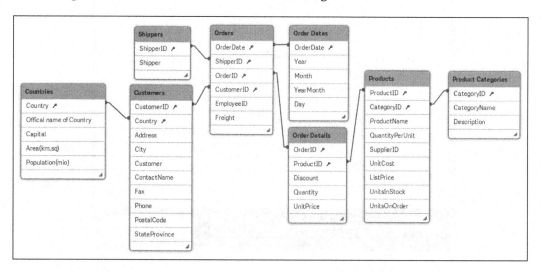

Data model viewer is an excellent tool to get an overview of the data model. It is also a very good debugging tool in the application development process.

Check that the data model looks the way you want it to and make sure that you have no circular references. Circular references will be marked with red links and synthetic keys will be named $Syn.

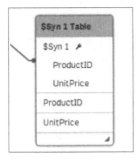

If the script execution creates a synthetic key, you will see this in the data model viewer.

Using preview mode

The **Data model viewer** option has a useful additional feature: preview mode. This mode allows you to preview both data and metadata of a field.

Select a field in a table and click on the **Preview** button to the lower-left corner of the screen. This opens the **Preview** panel in which you can see data about the field and some sample data records from the table. In addition, you can define dimensions and measures based on the chosen field, as shown in the following screenshot:

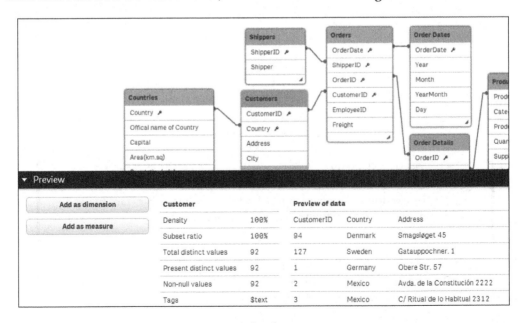

Data connectors

In addition to loading data from files, Qlik Sense can connect to databases using the ODBC and OLEDB interfaces. To see which databases you can connect to, you need to open **Data load editor** and click on **Create new connection**.

When you select **OLEDB** and then **Select provider**, you will see a list of the installed OLEDB providers. If your database isn't listed, you need to install the appropriate software from your database provider.

If you choose ODBC, you will see the defined data sources. However, you may still have drivers installed for which there are no data sources defined. To find out whether this is the case, you must open **ODBC Administrator** in Windows and look in the **Drivers** tab (as shown in the following screenshot). If your database isn't listed, you need to install the appropriate software from your database provider.

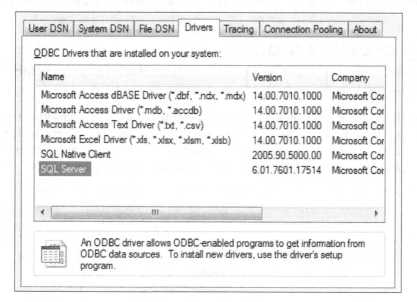

Windows ODBC Administrator

 The default ODBC administrator is opened by navigating to **Control Panel | Administrative tools | Data Sources (ODBC)** in Windows. However, on a 64-bit OS, you may also want to use 32-bit drivers. To manage these, you need to open C:\Windows\ SysWOW64\odbcad32.exe.

Once the ODBC driver is installed, you need to define a data source. We recommend that you do this on the **System DSN** tab in **ODBC Administrator**. When this is done, the data source will appear in the Qlik Sense ODBC dialog.

You can also use custom connectors with Qlik Sense, such as the Salesforce connector (as shown in the next screenshot) that you can download from the Qlik download page. These should be put in `C:\Program Files\Common Files\Qlik\Custom Data`. They will then appear in your list of connectors.

The list of connectors, including two custom connectors

The user interface – sheets and visualizations

Once you have loaded the data into Qlik Sense, it is time to create the visualizations in the graphical user interface. A basic set of sheets and visualizations should normally be supplied by the application developer, and additional ones can be created by the users themselves.

Creating a sheet

Perform the following steps to create a sheet:

1. Create an empty sheet from **App overview**, as shown in the next screenshot. So, if you have **Data load editor** open, you need to click on **App overview**:

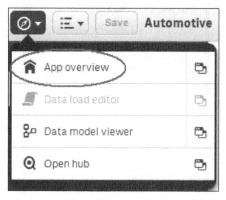

The App overview command

2. In **App overview**, you can create your first sheet by clicking on the sheet placeholder with a plus sign, as shown in the following screenshot:

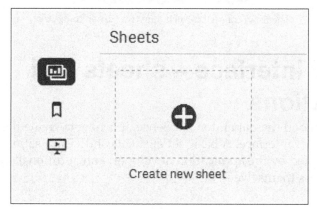

The Create new sheet button

3. Name it and hit *Enter*. You have now created an empty sheet and need to put some visualizations on it.

Adding visualizations

Perform the following steps to add visualizations:

1. Click on the newly created sheet. You are now looking at the empty sheet, but you have probably figured this out already, since the text **The sheet is empty** is located in the middle.

2. Click on the **Edit** button to the right in the toolbar to start adding things. Doing so will open the Assets panel to the left listing a number of object types: **Bar chart**, **Combo chart**, **Filter pane**, and so on. Now, you can drag and drop an object type onto your sheet, thereby creating such an object. If you, for instance, drag a bar chart onto the sheet, you will create an empty bar chart.

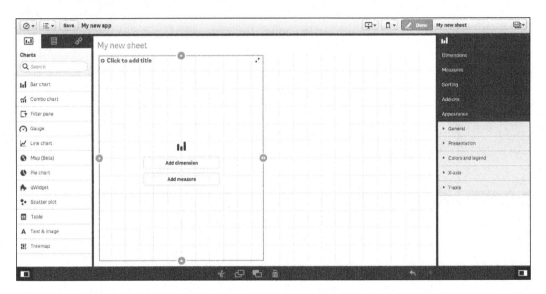

3. Depending on where you drop it, it will use all of the sheet or just half the sheet. Move the object around before you drop it, and you'll see. You can also adjust its size at a later stage.

4. Once you have dropped it, the bar chart will clearly show that it needs a dimension and a measure in order to display properly. You can click on the buttons on the bar chart to define these, but you can also use the Assets panel to the left.

The Assets panel shows object types, but if you look carefully, you will see that there are three tabs at its top: one for object types, one for fields, and one for the predefined library entities. So, if you click on the middle icon, you will see a list of fields that can be used as dimensions or as measures.

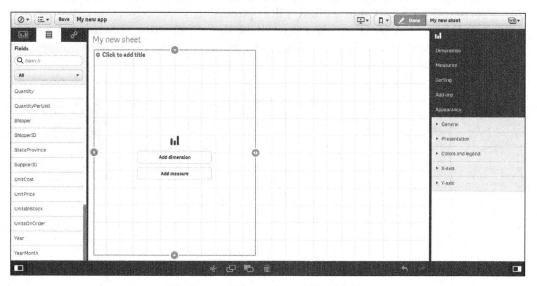

The Assets panel now shows a list of fields

Adding dimensions and measures

You can now drag and drop fields onto the bar chart, thereby creating the dimension and the measure.

A dimension is a field with discrete values, for example customer, product, or month. A chart will create one number per dimensional value; hence, a bar chart will create one bar per distinct value in the chosen field.

A measure is usually a number, for example, sum of sales or number of orders, and this will constitute the height of the bars.

When you drag a field onto the empty bar chart, Qlik Sense will ask you what you want to do with this field. You can add it (as a dimension), or you can use it inside an aggregation function (Sum(), Count(), or Min()) to form a measure.

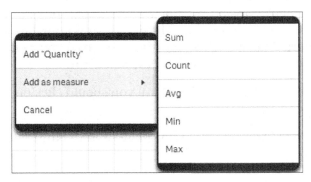

Adding measures

Defining bar charts

When you have added both dimension and measure, the bar chart will appear as shown in the next screenshot. To the right, you will have the properties of the bar chart, where you can set its properties: the sort order, the colors, and so on. You can also define the dimension and the measure directly in the chart properties.

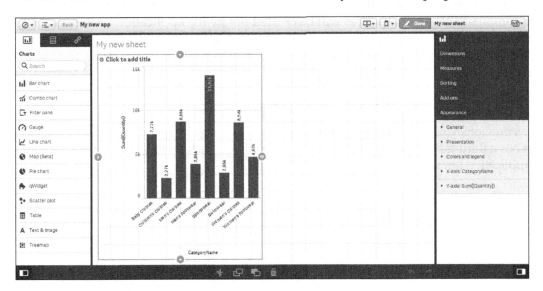

1. To see the final result, you need to click on **Done** in the toolbar, which takes you back to fullscreen.

   Clicking on the **Save** button in Qlik Sense Desktop will save the application as a file with the extension `.qvf` in the application folder (`C:\Users\<user>\Documents\Qlik\Sense\Apps`). The file contains both data and script and it can be imported to other Qlik Sense installations. However, you may need to adjust the script so that it runs from the new location.

2. When you are done with the bar chart, you should click on **Save** and start creating your next visualization.

In the server version of Qlik Sense, you don't have a **Save** button. The changes are saved automatically.

Storytelling

A new exciting feature in Qlik Sense is **storytelling**. Storytelling is basically a presentation mode where you can first prepare a presentation—like a slide show—and then present it. Storytelling is also an excellent way to present an application and create its overview.

When you create an application, you can of course also create a story that can be used by anyone who uses the application. However, we believe that the more common use case is that stories will be created not by the application developer, but rather by contributors—power users who choose to add elements to the application. Hence, storytelling is described in *Chapter 6, Contributing to Data Discovery*.

The application library

As previously mentioned, the Assets panel can show object types and fields. However, it has a third tab for predefined library entities. If you click on this tab, you will see the application library.

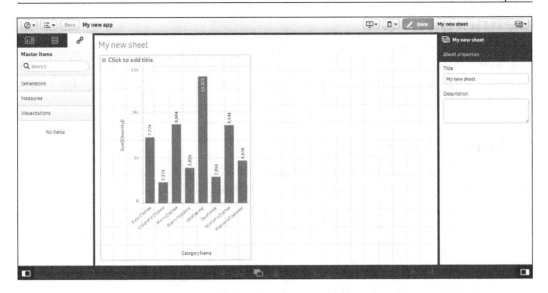

The library contains predefined entities that can simplify the Qlik Sense usage for a business user. Dimensions, measures, or entire visualizations can be stored in the library.

You do not *need* to use the library—nothing has to be predefined for Qlik Sense to work. However, if you want to reuse formulas or you have a situation where your task is to deliver an app to a business user, it is a good idea to use the library.

Which fields should be exposed?

Often, you have many fields in an app, of which only a few should be exposed as dimensions. Then, you should use the library to define the fields that are appropriate as dimensions and name them in a way that they can be easily understood.

A dimension can also be a group of exposed fields, a drill-down group, or a cyclic group. It can also be a formula using an `Aggr()` function that defines an array of values. In all these cases, it is a good idea to define the dimension in the library.

Defining KPIs

Measures are formulas that define KPIs. These are often used in many places in an app, so it is convenient to store the definition in one place only. Then, should you want to change the definition, you need to do it in the library only. Also, this is a way to ensure that there is only *one version of the truth*.

Creating library entries

Library entries can be created in several different ways. The most obvious way is to enter the library and click on the **Create new** button.

An alternative way is to do it from **Data model viewer**. Here, you can mark a field and click on the **Preview** button (in the bottom-left corner of the screen). You have the options of adding the field as dimension or measure.

Whichever way you choose to use when you create your dimension, you will see the following dialog where you define your dimensions:

The Create dimension dialog

When you create a measure, you will see the following dialog. Make sure that you have an aggregation function, for example `Sum()`, `Count()`, or `Min()`, wrapping the field reference.

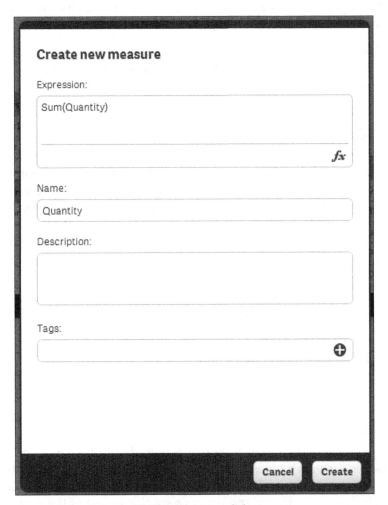

The Create measure dialog

Visualizations can only be entered into the library by the use of drag and drop, so you need to have created the visualization on the sheet first.

Best practices in data visualization

In the new world of ever increasing data volumes, the ability to visually communicate insights from data is an important skill set. Both the structure of an app and the chosen visualizations affect how data is perceived.

An app can contain many sheets, and the order of the sheets and what you put on them is the first consideration. Best practice can be summarized in three letters: **dashboard**, **analysis**, and **report** (**DAR**).

Dashboard

The dashboard is where the high-level perception takes place. It is usually the first sheet or the landing page, and it should give just the most important information and have the least amount of interactivity. Its main purpose is to help users get an overview and scan for status changes. The users can at a glance see whether things are working or not. It's a starting point, such as a table of contents; the user gets an idea of what is available and then heads off to other parts of the app based on what they have seen.

Some basic information about dashboards is as follows:

- Display data only on a high level
- Don't use too many KPIs
- Use no or very few filtering options
- The most important information should be large

Analysis

The analysis pages should be more interactive: they should help users explore the data and look for answers to questions they may have formed on the dashboard page. Analysis pages are where the user spends time and interacts with the data. Typically, each sheet has a theme and covers a specific aspect of the business. The analysis pages are where the user learns from data.

Here is some basic information about analysis pages:

- Allow filter panes or list boxes to facilitate selections
- Make sure an entire page is about a particular topic
- Use graphs

Reporting

The third type of sheet is the reporting sheet. It is not always necessary to have these, but often it is advantageous to gather the most granular information on dedicated sheets. This is the purpose of the reporting sheets: to give the most granular information with tabular data. This is where a user can spend a lot of time sorting and filtering through the details.

Here is some basic information about reporting sheets:

- Display transactional data in tabular form
- Give the users the ability to view every detail they need to take action on

Structuring a sheet

The structure within a sheet is also important. When you create an app, it's your job to prioritize information and display it in a way so the users better understand the data and find their way in the app.

The human eye scans most content in an **F** pattern. The first time we see a page, we read the first line, then a bit of the second line, and then work our way down the left-hand side of a page looking for keywords. This means that the content at the top of the page is the most important real-estate on a page, especially the top-left. The top of the sheet gives the users an idea of what content a page may contain and the scent of whether or not they are on the right track to finding what they are looking for. So, label the sheets appropriately.

It is also important that users easily find objects they are looking for. This applies to filter panes and listboxes, where the user makes selections. If used in several sheets, they should if possible be placed in the same place in all sheets. Further, given how a human eye scans the page, these objects should preferably be placed to the left.

Graphs and other visualizations

Visualization also includes choosing appropriate graphs. Getting the graph right is important; otherwise, the data can be misinterpreted. There are several highly regarded thought leaders who have written excellent reading material on this topic, for example, Edward Tufte and Stephen Few. If you have not read any book in this area and you intend to build business intelligence applications, we recommend that you do this. It will help you in your work.

Dimensions and measures

You should start by asking yourself, "What do I want to show?". The answer is usually sales, quantity, or some other number. This is your **measure**.

The second question you should ask yourself is, "How many times should this measure be calculated? Per what do I want to show this measure?". The answer could be once per month, once per customer, once per supplier, or something similar. This is your **dimension**.

The dimension and the measure of a chart are the core of the visualization and often indicate what visualization to choose. It is important to understand which type of field is used as dimension. For example, when showing trends over time, you should usually use a line chart or a bar chart. The same is also true for any dimension with an implicit, intrinsic order. By the same token, you should never use a line chart unless the dimension has an implicit order.

The fields used as dimensions can be classified into the following groups:

- **Nominals**: These are fields with qualitative values that *lack* intrinsic order, for example, product, customer, color, gender, and so on.

- **Ordinals**: These are fields with qualitative values that *have* intrinsic order, for example, ratings such as unsatisfied, neutral, or satisfied that have no numeric meaning.

- **Intervals**: These are fields with quantitative values that *lack* a natural zero. They are like coordinates, for example, date, time, longitude, temperature, and so on.

- **Ratios**: These are fields with quantitative values that *have* a natural zero. They are like amounts, for example, quantity, sales, profit, weight, and so on.

With this classification in mind, it is easier to describe what you can and cannot do with some graph types.

The bar chart

The most common visualization is the bar chart. Bar charts can be used for almost any dimension, and it is easy to compare the sizes of two bars. Further, they are good for ordinal data, since the intrinsic order can be used. This also means that trends over time can easily be spotted.

If a second measure is added to the bar chart, you will get two bar series so that you can make comparisons both between the measures and along the dimension. For example, in the following chart, you can compare not only the sales regions, but also the commercial vehicle sales with total sales:

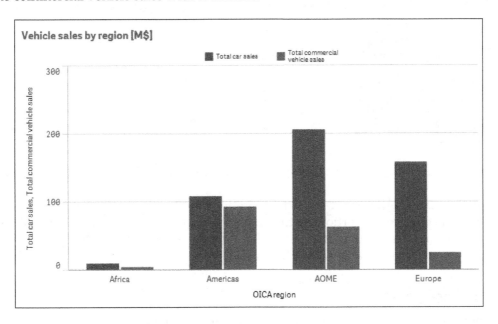

A bar chart is often the best visualization. By adding a second measure or a second dimension, you can get several series of bars.

The pie chart

The next visualization is the pie chart. This should only be used if the dimension is of the nominal type and you want to display the relative proportions. Pie charts are not good for ordinal data, since the order of the dimensional values isn't obvious. Pie charts are especially useful to convey an overview of the relative sizes. For instance, in the following pie chart, you can clearly see that the combined sales in USA and China constitute more than 50 percent—something that is not at all clear if you instead look at the corresponding bar chart:

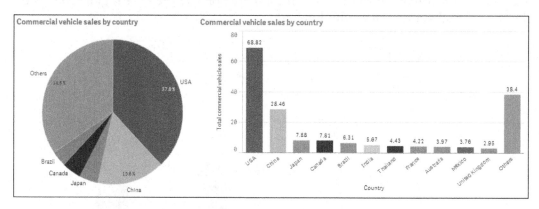

Normally, a bar chart is easier to read, but in this case the pie chart is better at showing the relative proportions of the largest countries. However, it can sometimes be hard to judge the relative sizes of the slices if there is only a small difference in between them. Then, a bar chart is a better choice.

The line chart

The next visualization is the line chart. This should only be used if the first dimension is of the interval type. Line charts are particularly useful for showing a change over time. Several lines can be used, either by using a second dimension or by adding measures.

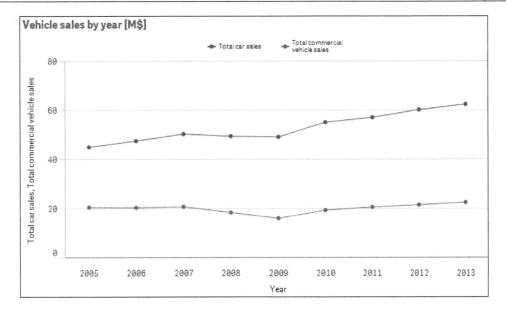

Line charts are good when you want to analyze trends over time.

The scatter chart

Scatter charts are good if you want to compare two different quantitative measures for the same dimension, that is, pairs of data per some dimension. Such plots are useful to find clusters of values, linear arrangements, gaps, and values that are much different from the norm. These are the kinds of patterns that are meaningful in correlation relationships.

The unique strength of this chart type is its ability to encode values along two quantitative scales used as two axes. Note that the logical dimension is *not* used as an axis. Instead, two *measures* are used as axes.

The dimension, which should normally be of the nominal type, defines the number of points in the scatter chart.

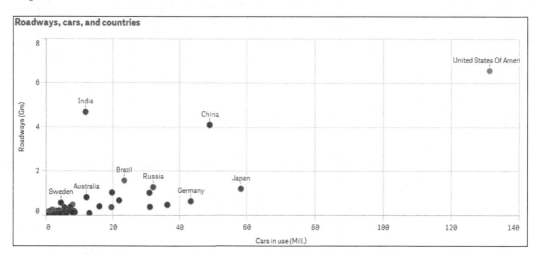

The preceding scatter chart shows the amount of roads per country (in million kilometers) versus the number of cars (in million units). The color indicates the country's population.

The tree map

Another chart type to mention is the tree map (called block chart in QlikView 11). This is an excellent visualization if you have two or more dimensions with a hierarchical relationship and one single measure. The reason why it is called tree map is that it was originally designed to display hierarchical relationships that have a structure like a tree. In Qlik Sense, you can use it for nonhierarchical relationships that have no resemblance with trees whatsoever. Again, the dimensions should be of the nominal type.

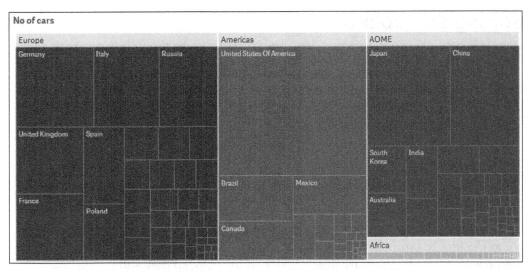

A tree map showing the number of cars in different countries

The geographical map

The last chart type to mention is the geographical map. This visualization is new in Qlik Sense, and you can display regions and areas on a map of a country or region. Also, here the dimension is of the nominal type.

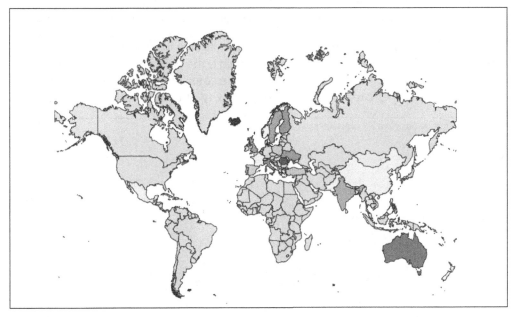

In Qlik Sense, you can connect maps to the data.

Sorting and colors

Once you have chosen the appropriate chart type, perform the following steps:

1. Choose the appropriate chart settings, for example, scale, sorting, and appearance. Nominals should be sorted alphabetically or by some form of measure, for example, the size of the bar. The other types should be sorted according to the intrinsic sort order.

2. You also need to label the chart, for example, add a title, descriptions, *y* axis units, and so on.

3. Finally, you should also make sure to use the appropriate colors, but be careful here.

Bright colors are beautiful, but when it comes to data visualization, it is best practice not to use highly saturated colors. Instead, it is good to tone it down a bit. The main reason is that lighter colors are much easier on the eyes, so they show data better for example when displayed on large screens. Further, bright colors draw attention, so they should only be used to highlight a specific field value or condition.

> The color should *never* be a decoration only. It should *always* carry information.

One way is to use the same color everywhere for the same field value. This way, the user will easily identify the corresponding bars or slices in multiple visualizations.

Another way is to use a color that has an intensity that is in proportion to a specific calculation. For instance, in the following bar chart, the bars indicate the total number of sold cars in different countries and the color intensity indicates the number of sold cars per capita. This is one good way of using colors.

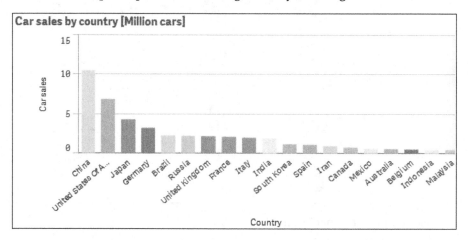

Migrating applications from QlikView to Qlik Sense

All QlikView applications since QlikView Version 8 can easily be migrated. However, the conversion is only partial: the data and the script will be converted, but nothing from the layout is used. Perform the following steps to migrate applications:

1. Move the QlikView app—the .qvw file—to your Qlik Sense Desktop app folder at `C:\Users\<user>\Documents\Qlik\Sense\Apps`. The file will then appear in your Desktop hub as a legacy app. Its name will have **(qvw)** after it:

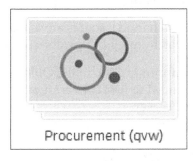

2. You can now open the app and see the data model and the existing script.

3. Once you make changes, you will need to save these; this is when the conversion takes place. The old app with the new changes will be saved into a file with extension .qvf, and the old .qvw file will be renamed to `*.qvw.backup`.

Changes to the script

Now, you must change the script. The structure of the script need not be changed, but all references to databases and files should be changed. In Qlik Sense, you need to use the data connections library. Hence, you must create the library entries that you need, and then replace connect strings and file references with references to the library.

Changes to the user interface

The modern layout in Qlik Sense with responsive design has very little to do with the old static layout in a QlikView app. A consequence is that you will need to recreate all objects: all charts, lists, and tables. In fact, you will often have to rethink your entire layout. If you are deploying your apps in an environment where users have tablets or smartphones, you would probably have had to do this anyway, since the old style QlikView apps display poorly on small screens.

The best way to do this is to have both Qlik Sense and QlikView displaying the same app simultaneously. Then you can go through the app sheet by sheet and decide how to design your new Qlik Sense app.

The syntax for formulas has not changed, so it is advisable to use copy and paste when moving complex formulas from QlikView objects into Qlik Sense objects.

Currently, there is no support for migration in the Qlik Sense server. So, if you want your old app on a server, you need to first convert it using Qlik Sense Desktop and then import the new file to the server.

Publishing your apps

When you have created an app, the next step is to make it available for other users. Perform the following steps if you have developed your app using Qlik Sense Desktop:

1. Import the app using the **Apps** sheet in the Qlik Sense Management Console. There, you will find an **Import** button in the top-right corner.

Name	Owner	Published	Stream	Tags
Equity Sales Analysis	hic (QTSEL\hic)			
Executive Dashboard	hic (QTSEL\hic)			
License Monitor	sa_repository (INTERNAL\sa_repository)	2014-09-08 12:47	Administration	
MFA Interactive	hic (QTSEL\hic)			
MFA Pharma Interactive	hic (QTSEL\hic)			
My new app	hic (QTSEL\hic)			
Operations Monitor	sa_repository (INTERNAL\sa_repository)	2014-09-08 12:47	Administration	

2. Once the file is imported, you may also need to assign the correct owner: mark the file, click on **Edit**, and change the owner if necessary. The file will then appear under **My Work** in the Qlik Sense hub.

> If you have developed the app using the server version, it will already be under **My Work**.

3. Before you publish the app, it is recommended that you make a copy of the file. Mark the file on the **Apps** page in the Qlik Sense Management Console and select **Duplicate** in the **More Actions** menu.

4. Now, you are ready to publish. You can publish the app by marking the file and clicking on the **Publish** button.

   Publishing means that you move an app from your personal workspace to a stream, which means that the file can be accessed by many people. The properties of the stream, including security rules, will then be applied. Note that the file will be removed from your personal workspace. This is the reason why it might be a good idea to make a copy of it.

   You will then be prompted to choose a stream for your use:

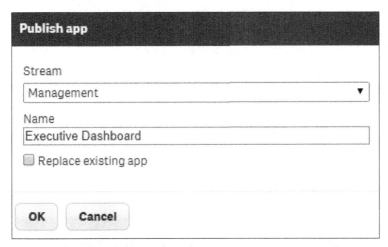

The Publish app dialog

Currently, there is no way to "unpublish" an app; if you want to remove it from a stream, you need to delete the app.

Visualization extensions

All objects in the Qlik Sense user interface are created with standard web technologies and use the standardized API to communicate with other parts of the product. This means that it is straightforward to create your own visualizations—given that you are familiar with programming and HTML5. Such visualizations are called **extensions**.

There are a number of extensions available that can be downloaded from the Internet. If you download extensions and want to use them with Qlik Sense Desktop, you should put them in `C:\Users\<user>\Documents\Qlik\Sense\Extensions`. If you want to use them in the Qlik Sense server, you need to import them using the Qlik Sense Management Console.

Once you have done this, the extensions will appear in the assets panel to the left when you edit a sheet.

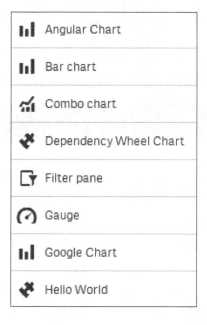

The Assets panel will display both the standard objects and extensions.

Using Workbench

If you want to create your own visualization, Workbench is a good place to start. Just start your Qlik Sense Desktop, open an Internet browser, and go to `http://localhost:4848/Workbench`.

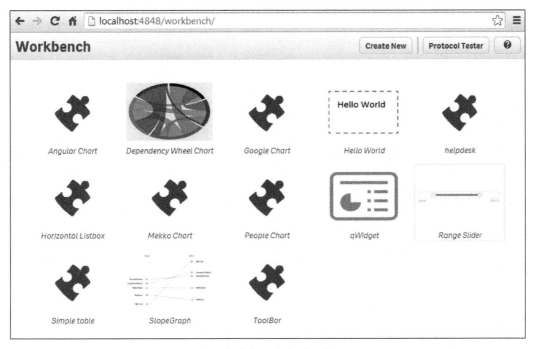

The Qlik Sense Workbench

This will open a web page that allows you to create extensions and edit the existing ones. If you click on **Create new**, you will be prompted for a name and on which template it should be based.

Once the visualization is created, you can edit all the files through this user interface: the JavaScript code, the CSS file, and the metadata.

Summary

In this chapter, we looked at the functions and commands you need to know to build engaging applications—both from a process perspective and, more practically, what you need to do to create an inviting user interface.

In the next chapter, we'll move away from app creation and start examining how a Qlik Sense server is managed and configured.

8
Administering Qlik Sense

Having established how to develop attractive and engaging applications with Qlik®️ Sense, it's time to turn our attention from authors and business users. Instead, we will consider the requirements of administrators. In this chapter, we will move away from data and analysis to what's needed to run a Qlik®️ Sense installation.

In this chapter, you will find information about the following topics:

- Architecture
- Clustering and nodes
- Licenses and tokens
- Streams and security concepts

The Qlik Sense architecture

Qlik Sense has an architecture that is different from the QlikView®️ Server architecture. Some components are very similar; others are very different. Hence, even if you know the QlikView architecture, you need to look at the following sections. In them, you will find an overview of some of the concepts in Qlik Sense.

Services

When you install the Qlik Sense server, you will install five services. These are the cornerstones of the architecture. They can be deployed in different ways to suit different deployment purposes.

The Qlik Sense services are as follows:

- **Qlik Sense Engine Service (QIX)**: This is the application service, which handles all application calculations and logic. Everything that concerns the data analysis is handled by this service.

- **Qlik Sense Proxy Service (QPS)**: This manages the Qlik Sense authentication, session handling, and load balancing.

- **Qlik Sense Repository Service (QRS)**: This manages persistence and the synchronization of licensing, security, and service configuration data.

- **Qlik Sense Repository Database (QRD)**: This service runs a relational database used by the QRS.

- **Qlik Sense Scheduler Service (QSS)**: This manages the scheduled reloads of Qlik Sense apps as well as other types of events, for example, task chaining.

In a standard installation, all five services run on the same computer, and this works fine as long as the load on the server doesn't become too heavy.

The services can run under any account, but should preferably run under an account dedicated to the Qlik Sense services.

Clients

Qlik Sense has two different clients: the hub and the management console (QMC).

The hub is used to access, edit, and publish apps. It always runs in a web browser, regardless of whether you use a desktop computer, tablet, or smartphone to access it.

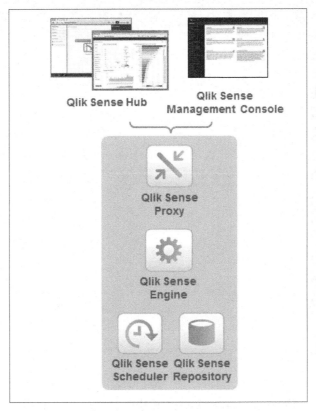

The basic Qlik Sense architecture

Qlik Management Console (QMC) is used for all types of administration. QMC is a web page found at `https://<computer_name>/qmc/`.

A link to this is installed in your Start menu during the installation.

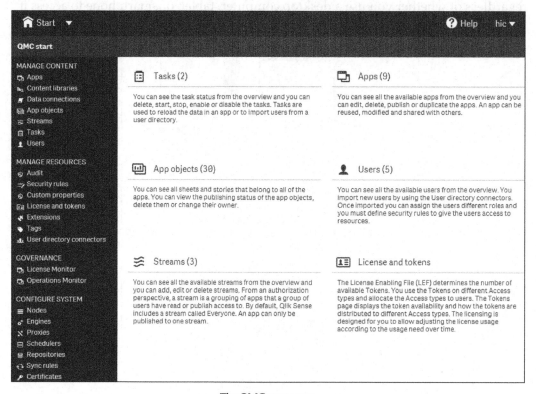

The QMC start page

In QMC, you can manage and monitor everything for your installation: apps, streams, security, users, and so on.

To the left, you have the four main groups: tools to manage the content, tools to manage resources, tools to monitor, and tools to configure the system.

It is important to understand that QMC is a multiuser environment, designed for the delegation of administration of, for example, streams to authors, if this fits a company's work process.

Applications

The apps are subject-specific; files that contain data, prepared visualizations, load script, and so on. This is where the analysis is done. From a user's perspective, an app is organized into sheets, sheet objects (visualizations), bookmarks, and stories. An app can be private or published to a stream.

If you want to access an app to do analysis, you can access it through the hub. However, if you want to perform any administrative task, such as importing or publishing an app, you can do it through QMC.

Nodes

Qlik Sense's site has an architecture that allows a distributed deployment. In other words, you can have several computers, each with a Qlik Sense installation, that work together and are managed as one coherent server. In such a configuration, each computer is called a **node** and the entire installation is called a **cluster**.

The installation can be configured so that data is synchronized between the different nodes, and so that the appropriate server is used for the client request. The purpose is, of course, to increase the system resilience and deployment flexibility.

Streams

The next important concept in Qlik Sense is **streams**. A stream is a dynamic, collaborative workgroup that is used when publishing applications. Hence, when you publish an app to a stream, you publish to a group of people.

A stream has members, security rules, and tags. It enables the user to read or publish apps, sheets, and stories. The users who have publishing rights to a stream create the content for that specific stream, and the users who have read access are the consumers of the apps.

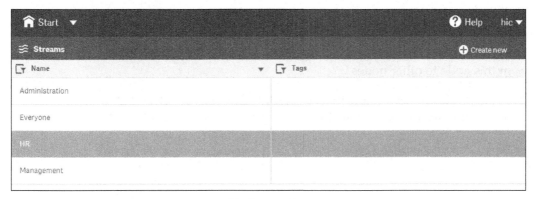

The Streams sheet

Deployment and licensing

Deploying a Qlik Sense server is usually straightforward, but there are still a couple of things to think of. The first question is about clustering.

Single node or multinode?

Normally, you should just install the Qlik Sense server making sure that it is set as a central node during the installation. Then, you will get a single node installation. However, sooner or later you need to ask yourself a question about clustering: how many servers do you want in your cluster? This book is not a comprehensive guide to clustering issues; it will only point out the basics and the questions you need to ask.

In a standard installation, all five services run on the same computer, and this works fine as long as the load on the server doesn't become too heavy. However, as soon as your installation starts to grow, you may need more computers to handle the load. If so, you can set up a cluster so that you have additional computers running only some of the services, and still manage the entire cluster as if it were only one computer.

By far the most common case is that Qlik Sense has a very large load, either due to many users or because some applications are large. Then, it might be a good idea to add one or several computers and use a separate Qlik Sense engine on each computer.

Another case is that you have several physical locations and want one node in each location, with the same content on each node. This way, the users always use the local node.

One of the computers must be set as the central node, that is, as the master. Here, you enter your license key and manage the entire cluster. Data will be synchronized from this node to other nodes.

It is possible to use the same entry point—the Qlik Sense proxy—for the entire cluster so that users don't notice that there are, in fact, several computers.

On the central node, it is recommended that you have a dedicated QPS and QIX that are used specifically for the QMC and not for the hub.

In addition, the central node must have the QSS installed even if other nodes with schedulers are added. This is because the scheduler on the central node is considered to be the master scheduler, which coordinates all scheduler activities within the site.

Hence, when defining your deployment strategy, you should try to answer some questions:

- What is the estimated number of computers needed to handle the number of apps and users you expect?
- Should the users use the same proxy so that you can set up rules for load balancing? Or should they use different entry points in the different locations?
- Do you want/need separate computers that are only used to run jobs, for example, to refresh the apps?

The answers will help you decide whether you should build a cluster of Qlik Sense servers. If you don't know, or if it is your first server in a cluster, you should just install the Qlik Sense server making sure that it is set as the central node during the installation.

License and access passes

The first thing you need to do after installing Qlik Sense is to enter the license key and make sure that you get a valid **License Enabling File** (**LEF**) from the Qlik license activation server. However, this is not enough to get going. You also need to assign a license to yourself. Alternatively, to express this in the correct terminology, you need to allocate *a token as a user access pass for yourself*.

This is done by navigating to **License and tokens | User access**. Here, you can click on the **Allocate** button, select a user, and click on **Allocate**. This means that you have given this user "unlimited" access to the Qlik Sense server. "Unlimited" means unlimited from a license perspective—you may still have restrictions on this user from a security perspective.

User access has been granted to the user hic

Tokens

The reason for this procedure is Qlik Sense's flexible licensing model. In the old license model, you bought Named CALs or some other license from Qlik, and that was then the license you had. To convert from one type of CAL to another was not possible, unless you contacted Qlik.

In the new model, you instead decide how you want to allocate the licenses you bought. Some are allocated to the equivalent of a Named CAL, while some are allocated to another license type. As a consequence, you don't buy licenses. Instead you buy **tokens**, which is a kind of currency that you can convert into licenses at a later stage. In the initial configuration, no tokens are assigned to be used and hence, the need to allocate a token to yourself.

Another consequence is that the terminology has changed. A Named CAL is no longer called Named CAL. Instead, it is called user access pass. So in the preceding case, you have effectively given yourself a Named CAL.

The Qlik Sense user access pass—and the QlikView Named CALs for that matter—is a general unlimited license that should be given to frequent users, that is, users that analyze data regularly, many times every month.

In Qlik Sense, there is a second license type that is designed to cover the needs of infrequent users. It is similar to the Usage CAL that exists in QlikView. It is called **login access pass**. A login access pass is equivalent to one login per month, that is, the login counter is refreshed so that a new login is possible every 28th day.

You can create login access passes in batches of 10, and 10 login access passes cost 1 token. These 10 logins can be used any way you want. They can, for example, be used by 10 different people that log in once per month or by one single user who logs in 10 times every month.

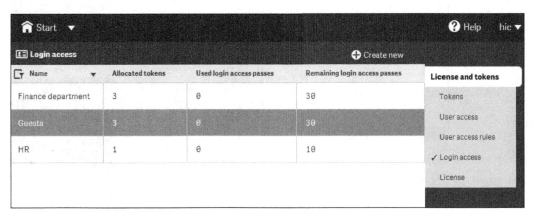

Login access passes can be created in pools for different groups of people

Access rules

Typically, you would use several tokens to create a pool of logins that can be dedicated for a group of people within your domain. You can create access rules both for user access passes and login access passes, and you should do this for your own benefit. This means that you can, for instance, say that anyone in the Finance department will get a user access pass when logging on, whereas the users of another department will share the login access passes of a specific pool.

Hence, when you create the user and login accesses you want, you can get an overview of the **Tokens** page, where you can clearly see the number of used tokens and how many you have left to allocate.

You can clearly see how many tokens you allocated to licenses, and how these are distributed over the two access types in the following screenshot:

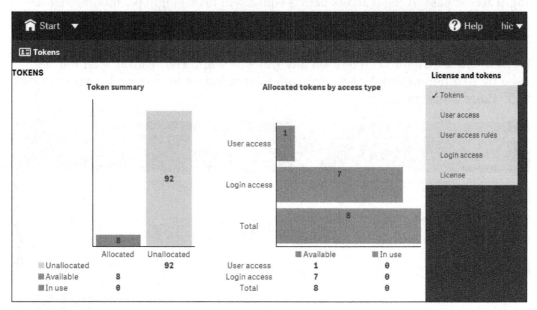

The Tokens screen in QMC

Management and monitoring

So far, this chapter has dealt with managing the installation and the licenses, but very little has been mentioned about the real purpose of the Qlik Sense administration, which is how to handle data and the analysis of data. In other words, how to handle applications, users, data connections, distribution, and so on. This section will cover these areas.

Importing and managing apps

Once the Qlik Sense server is deployed, perform the following steps:

1. Import an app that you created in Qlik Sense Desktop. This is something that you can do in the **Apps** sheet. Look for the **Import** button in the upper-right corner of the screen.

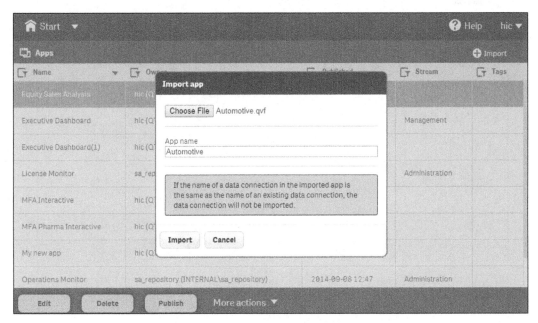

Importing an app created in Qlik Sense Desktop in the Apps screen

2. Once imported, you can set the owner of the app. Then, it will appear in the **My work** area in the hub of the owner. However, the app is still not published, which means that other users cannot see it.

3. When you publish it, you move the app from **My work** to another stream, and once it is published, its layout is fixed and cannot be changed.

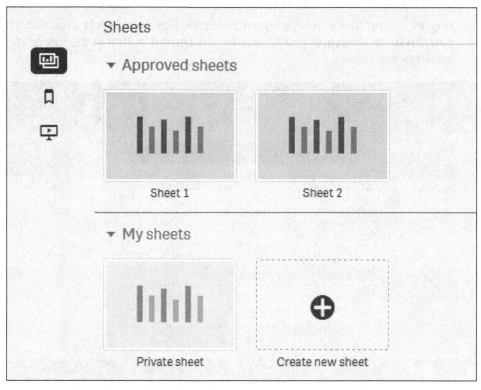

Once an app is published, the app overview in the hub changes

This is obvious if you look at the app overview in the hub. Here, you now have two rows of sheets: one with sheets that are fixed and public, and another with private sheets that aren't visible to other people.

You can also see this difference on the sheet listing the app objects. This sheet lists all sheets and stories, and QMC clearly indicates whether an object is public and who the owner is.

The user who creates an app is automatically designated as the owner of the app and its app objects. The app objects are published when the app they belong to is published. However, the users can add private app objects to the apps and share them by publishing the app objects from Qlik Sense. When this is done, the app overview in the hub gets three rows of sheets, as shown in the following screenshot:

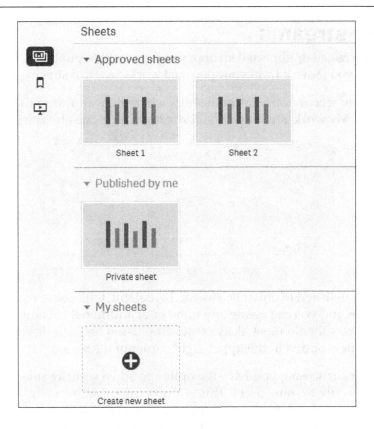

Users and user directories

As soon as you want to manage the Qlik Sense server in terms of ownership and access rights, you need to have your users defined. Normally, these are already defined in a user directory, for example, in Windows Active Directory. Hence, you want to reuse these definitions.

On the **User directory connectors** page, you can define several sources for your users and user groups. You need to do this and sync at least one of them before you can start distributing licenses and access rights to your user groups.

The users are managed on the **Users** sheet. However, when you first start Qlik Sense, the list of users is fairly short: just you and a couple of system users. To populate the list of users, you have two options:

- Define a user directory connector and sync the users in it
- Define rules for the access passes, so that the users can assign licenses to themselves without you having to do it

Defining streams

Once you have created or imported an app, you may want to publish it. Publishing an app means that you move it from your personal workspace to a stream of your choice.

You have already seen the streams in the hub, where they appear to the left as groups of apps. **My work** is your personal stream that no one else can see.

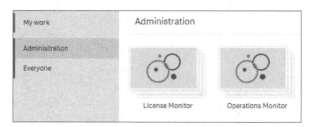

Streams, as seen from the hub

An app can be published to only one stream. By default, Qlik Sense includes a stream called **Everyone**, and you can create any number of additional streams from the **Streams** sheet. You should most likely create one stream for each distinct user group. Use the **Create new** button in the upper-right corner of the screen.

When creating your stream, you have the option to add a security rule, making the stream available only to some users. This is a very important security feature. One obvious example is if you have a set of apps that should be seen only by the Human Resources department. Then, you should create a stream for this group and use the user information from the directory service to give access to this stream.

Another common case is if you want to delegate the administration of a stream to a group of users. The following screenshot shows a security rule that grants access to the Human Resources stream and to all users belonging to the HR user directory:

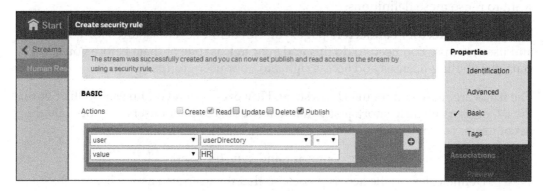

Connectivity management

Connectivity means the connection to source data. Source data can be ERP systems of different kinds, file folders, web addresses containing tables, and so on. When running a Qlik Sense script, data is pulled from the different sources into the Qlik Sense app, so that it can be analyzed at a later stage.

With Qlik Sense, it is easy to get an overview of all data connections used, something that used to be a challenge. By opening the **Data Connections** sheet, you get a list of the data connections used in the different apps.

The data connections can be managed and security can be set separately for the different connections. It is, for example, possible to prevent some users from using a specific data connector. This way, you can control the usage and ensure that data is used in the correct way.

Tasks

On the **Tasks** page, you define the jobs that need to run in the background. These are of two kinds: **reload tasks** and **user synchronizations**.

The reload tasks are necessary to refresh data in the apps, which means that you need to set up tasks so that they are refreshed with the frequency you want. Most apps should be refreshed once a day, but some others only need to be refreshed once a month. There are both advantages and disadvantages with a frequent refresh of the data. If it is refreshed rarely, for example, once per month, the users will not have the latest data.

On the other hand, if you refresh data too often, such as once per hour, you will have a heavy load on your server handling the reload tasks. You will also create a situation where two users in a meeting may have different opinions about what the correct number for a specific KPI is, since they looked at two different versions of the app. One looked at the app an hour ago, and the other just 10 minutes ago. This does not create an understanding; rather, it creates confusion, since you have two "versions" of the truth.

You should ask yourself if the users benefit most from having as fresh data as possible, or if they benefit more from having "one truth". A good balance is to have one refresh per day. The users will learn this, and refer to the numbers as "today's numbers" and "yesterday's numbers".

User synchronization is necessary to refresh data from the directory service, so that Qlik Sense is aware of any changes made to groups and users.

A task can be triggered by either a scheduler or the completion of another task. This way, you can get task chaining.

System management

The group to the bottom-left in QMC relates to system settings. Here, you can configure the nodes, engines, proxies, schedulers, repositories, sync rules, and certificates. With these, you can configure how the Qlik Sense server would work on different computers. You can do really advanced things here, but this is outside the scope of this book.

Security rules

You can set access control for most of the preceding settings, for example, only some users should be able to see a specific application; only some users should be allowed to use a specific data connection; all users should be allowed to create data connectors to databases, but not to file folders; only some users are allowed to log in using a specific pool of login access passes; and so on.

When doing so, you should think of the following user types:

- **Developer**: These are users who are allowed to create apps, sheets, stories, objects, and who can use and create data connections
- **Contributor**: These are users who are allowed to create stories and sheets for published apps but are not allowed to create new apps
- **Consumer**: These are users who can only use apps, sheet, stories, objects, and so on and are not allowed to create content

These rules are called security rules, even though they do not always pertain to true security. They can be edited on each sheet, for example, the rules for streams can be edited on the **Streams** sheet, but there is also an overview: the security rules have a sheet of their own.

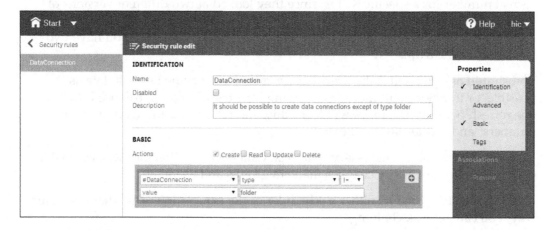

When you create a security rule using the basic interface, you create a property-value pair that grants users the right to do something. In the preceding screenshot, all users are granted the right to create data connections that aren't file folders.

The rules are property-based and the properties are used to describe the parties involved in an access request. In the usual case, the parties involved are the user making the request, the environment the request is made from, and the resource the request applies to.

Each property is defined in a property-value pair such as **group = Sales** or **resourcetype = App**. Each request, in turn, includes the property-value pairs for the users, environments, and resources involved in the request together with the action that the the person making the request wishes to perform on the resource, for example create, update, or delete.

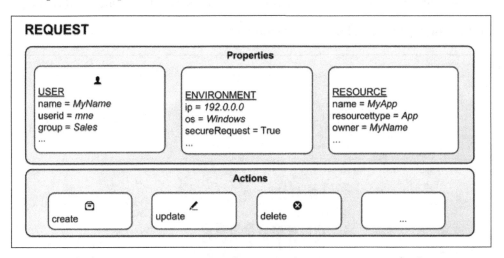

The four components in security rules: user, environment, resource, and action

You can create rules based on the property-value pairs. This means that requests for an action on a resource are granted only if the property value of the requester matches the property-value conditions defined in a security rule for that resource.

A rule can read as a sentence in the following way: *Allow the requester to [action] the [resource] provided that [conditions].*

Each rule must describe the action and the resource or resources the action should be applied to. If you don't define any rules for a resource, no users will have access to that resource.

By design, security rules are written to include, not exclude, users. Users who are not included in security rules will be denied access. So, security rules must be created to enable users to interact with Qlik Sense content, data connections, and other resources.

Hence, the rules define when access is granted, and there is no rule that can deny a user access. If there is a rule that allows the user to do something, they are allowed to do so. So if you want to deny a user something, you must delete the rule that grants access, or edit the rule.

Monitoring

Delivered together with Qlik Sense, you will also find two monitoring Qlik Sense applications: **License Monitor** and **Operations Monitor**. These read the logfiles of Qlik Sense and will give you a good overview of the state of the Qlik Sense server.

The following screenshot shows **Operations Monitor**:

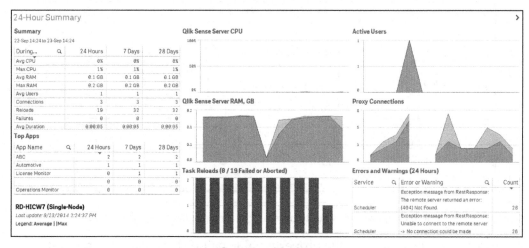

Operations Monitor

The following screenshot shows **License Monitor**:

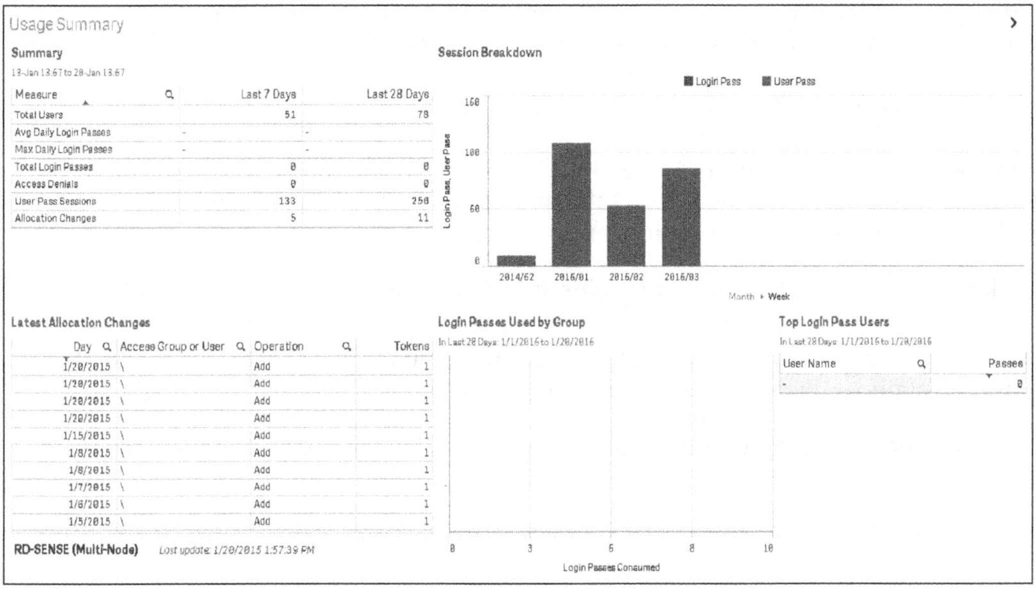

Lincense Monitor

Security

The security in Qlik Sense consists of many parts. In QMC, there is a system with security rules for almost everything you can do, not only data access; it also has the rights to change the setup or publish apps or sheets. This implies protection of the platform, that is, how the Qlik Sense platform itself is protected and how it communicates and operates.

However, security, as a concept, goes beyond that. So let's start from the beginning.

Authentication and authorization

The two most basic concepts in security are authentication and authorization. Authentication answers this question: who is the user and how can the user prove it? Authorization answers this question: what does this specific user have access to, and what are they allowed to do?

In Qlik Sense, authentication and authorization are two distinct, unconnected actions. In addition, the sources of information used for authentication do not have to be the same as for authorization, and vice versa.

Qlik Sense uses standard authentication protocols (for example, Integrated Windows Authentication, HTTP headers, and ticketing) to authenticate every user requesting access. If you want a customized authentication, you can configure this in the proxy, but the details of this are outside the scope of this book.

Authorization is the procedure of granting or denying user access to resources, but this can be done on several levels:

- First, there is the administrator access control. Which rights are needed for the different roles and responsibilities of the administrators? This is controlled in the security rules as previously described.

- Secondly, there is the app level authorization: is the user allowed to access the app? Which functions in the app is the user allowed to use (for example, printing, exporting, and snapshots)?

Content security

Content security is a critical aspect of setting up and managing your Qlik Sense system. QMC enables you to centrally create and manage security rules for all your Qlik Sense resources. Security rules define what a user is allowed to do with a resource, for example, read, update, create, or delete.

Additionally, there is data reduction by a section access in the script. For example, with data level authorization, is the user allowed to see all of the data or just parts of it? The section access is an app-defined, data-driven security model, intimately connected with the data model. It allows the implementation of row- and field-level data security.

In data level authorization, the authentication information also exists in the data model (albeit in a hidden part of it). It could be, for example, a username.

The selection propagates to all the other tables in the standard QlikView manner, so that the appropriate records in all tables are excluded, wherein Qlik Sense reduces the scope for this user to only the possible records. This way, the user will only see data pertaining to the countries to which they are associated.

Summary

In this chapter, we have seen that with QMC, you can manage a Qlik Sense installation very efficiently. It includes a wide range of functions that allow you to configure your system the way you want it, and it allows you to set access rights on not only apps, but also on streams, licenses, and data connectors.

Since QMC is based on standard web technology, you can, in principle, use any browser to run it, and it integrates well with other systems used to manage software and hardware components. In addition, you can use APIs to create custom management utilities.

To end this book, we'll be looking at putting Qlik Sense into practice for active data discovery, as we spend the last chapters analyzing the examples of sales, HR, travel expenses, and demographics.

9
Sales Discovery

Throughout this book, we have shared the driving forces in the creation of Qlik® Sense and key capabilities to aid in helping organizations make better business decisions. This chapter is the first of four that will apply Qlik Sense to the challenges of analyzing sales performance within your organization. This example and many others are available for you to explore live at http://sense-demo.qlik.com. Please bookmark this link as additional demonstrations and examples are constantly being added and updated. Now let's turn our attention to the following challenge of sales analysis and how Qlik Sense addresses this common business challenge.

In this chapter, we will cover the following topics:

- Common sales analysis problems
- The unique way Qlik Sense addresses these problems
- How the **Sales Discovery** application was built

The business problem

Analyzing sales information can be a difficult process for any organization, and is critical to meeting sales expectations and understanding customer demand signals. What makes sales analysis so difficult is that many perspectives can be taken on the enormous amount of information that is captured during the sales process.

Some key questions can include:

- Who are our top customers?
- Who are our most productive sales representatives?
- How are our high margin products selling and to whom?

The key thing here is that during the analysis process, one answered question always leads to further questions depending on the results; in other words, the analysis process's diagnostics. These paths to discovery cannot be precalculated or anticipated. With this in mind, let's take a look at how the **Sales Discovery** application seeks to meet these requirements.

Application features

Qlik Sense's associative model allows users to answer the common questions outlined in the preceding section through the selection of elements in filter boxes, but more importantly, drive follow-up questions. Often, this relies on Qlik Sense's ability to instantly identify the associated and nonassociated data, which is also known as "The Power of Gray" after the color assigned to nonassociated elements highlighted in *Chapter 5, Empowering Next Generation Data Discovery Consumers*. The following are two key beginner questions that will drive additional questions as the analysis begins.

Key questions can include:

- Who are our top customers?
    - What are these customers buying?
    - Where are these customers buying from?
    - Are the products getting there?
    - Who are our bottom five customers?

- Can we cross-promote products?
    - Who are our most productive sales representatives?
    - What products are the most productive sales representatives selling?
    - Whom are they selling to?
    - Which regions are they being sold in?

Before we begin, let's review the main sheets in the **Sales Discovery** application. As noted in the following screenshot, the application is made up of the **Performance Dashboard**, **Top Customers**, **Shipments**, **Sales and Margin**, **US Regional Analysis**, **Transactions**, and finally, **Past Dues** sheets:

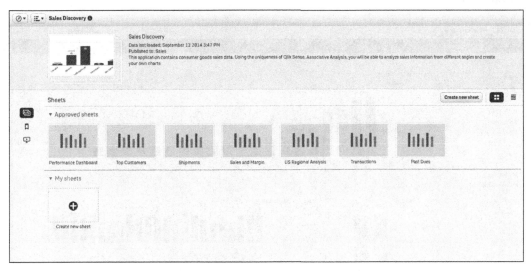

The application overview

Given the nature of the associative model, all filters are global, allowing a user to explore each application sheet in the context of the selected filters and associative results. Filters serve as a way to ask questions to the Qlik Sense application.

Who are our top customers?

So with that said, let's begin with our first question, "Who are our top customers?". This is a typical question that can be handled by a number of BI solutions in the marketplace.

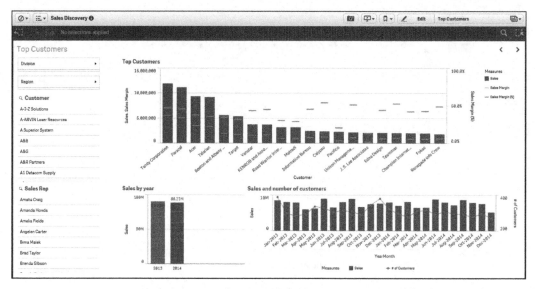

Our top customers

In the preceding screenshot, we can see that the top five customers in terms of sales are **Tandy Corporation**, **Paracel**, **Acer**, **Talarian**, and **Boston and Albany Railroad Company**.

360-degree customer view

Now is where things get interesting in Qlik Sense and the associative experience. Once we select these customers, as seen in the following screenshot, we get a 360-degree view of them across the application. Immediately, we can see which representatives have sold to these accounts, the trended revenue, year-on-year sales, as well as what percentage of the regions these sales were made. The percentage of the regions (noted by the green arrow) where the sales where made is highlighted in the filter list shade, which shows approximately 25 percent of the regions:

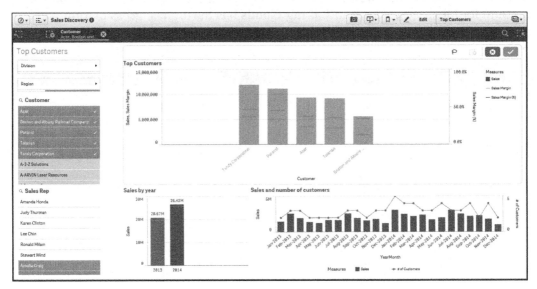

Top five customer sales

Filtering customers

The preceding information leads naturally to the next question: what are these customers buying and from where?

Again, because of Qlik's associative indexing engine, this information is linked together automatically. Based on this, let's view the impact that filtering these top five customers has on sales and gross margins, as shown in the following screenshot. Note that the customer filter box with selections is globally available at the top of the screen. In the **Sales and Margin** sheet, we can see that **Canned Foods** and **Produce** account for the largest sales, and **Baking Goods** has the highest gross margin with just over 50 percent.

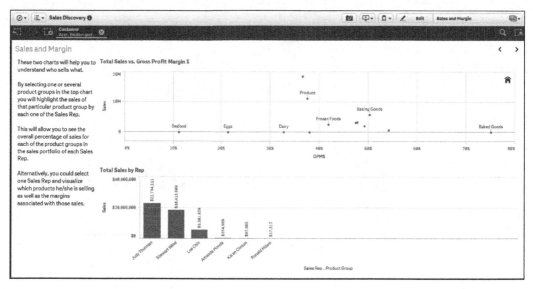

What are these customers buying?

As we continue our analysis, the next question that is most likely to arise is where are these sales occurring? Again, this data is available in the sales transaction, and Qlik's associative indexing engine makes this easily available and interactive within the application. Note that in the next figure, the **US Regional Analysis** sheet displays the sales by states, customers, and the important shipments as well:

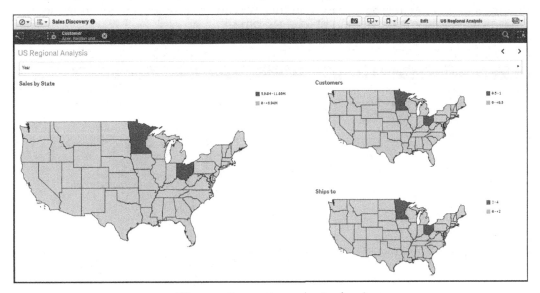

Where are these customers buying from?

Reviewing shipments for top customers

We can see in the preceding screenshot that Minnesota and Ohio account for all top five customers sales that are between 5.94 million and 11.89 million. After reviewing this sheet, a number of questions can arise and be analyzed. Let's follow one specific thought on shipments. Are products getting there?

As we know, shipments play a critical role in a sales process because without shipping, you cannot book revenue and continue to grow sales. With this in mind, let's turn our attention to the **Shipments** sheet as shown in the following screenshot. From here, we can see the trending shipment information on two levels: % **On time shipments** and **Number of shipments late vs on time**. Additionally, we see that the on time shipment goal is **86%**. Based on this, we can see problems in meeting these goals in September, October, and November 2014:

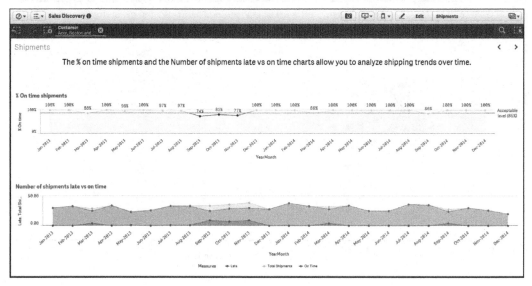

Are the products getting there?

Reviewing the bottom five customers

Now, let's turn our attention to an equally important topic: who are our bottom five customers and how can we increase sales to them? In the following screenshot, we can see the bottom five customers: **Edna Design**, **Teammax**, **Champion International**, **Fokas**, and **Renegade Info Crew**. Our sales to them are 2 million products or less and they purchase lower margin products:

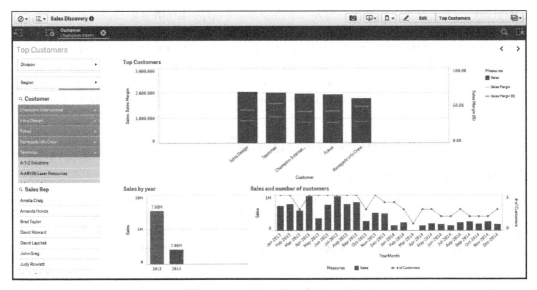

Who are our bottom five customers?

Noting this, let's dig in a bit deeper on the products they purchase. In the following screenshot, we can see that these customers purchase a large amount of **Produce** and **Snack Foods**. Now, the question arises—can we cross-promote products to increase our sales from these customers?

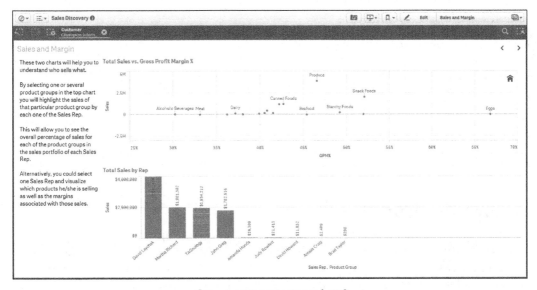

Can we cross-promote products?

Based on the information gleaned, we can see some opportunities to cross-promote products. For example, with the high purchase of **Produce** by these customers, perhaps a cross-promotional program that introduces **Eggs** (at a **67**% margin) to them to supplement their produce may raise sales. Additionally, with strong sales of **Snack Foods**, perhaps we can expand the sales of **Baked Goods** (at a **52**% margin) to these customers as well. Now let's turn our attention to the analysis of sales representatives.

Who are our most productive sales representatives?

As often is the case, a key area for analysis is the performance of sales representatives. So, let's turn our attention to the **Sales and Margin** sheet in our **Sales Discovery** application, as shown in the following screenshot. Here, we can see that **Judy Thurman**, **Steward Wind**, and **Lee Chin** lead the sales team in revenue terms:

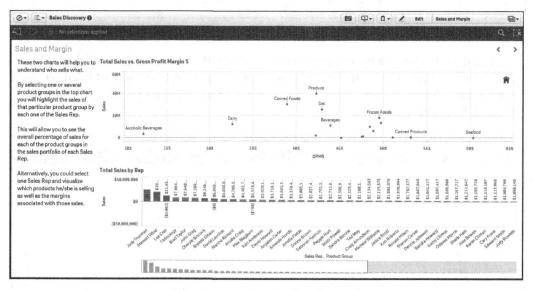

Who are our most productive sales reps?

Analyzing products

The next question that arises is what products are they selling? As we can see, **Canned Foods** and **Produce** are the top selling products. After identifying these sales representatives and top selling products, we will need to combine this information with an understanding of which customers are driving these sales.

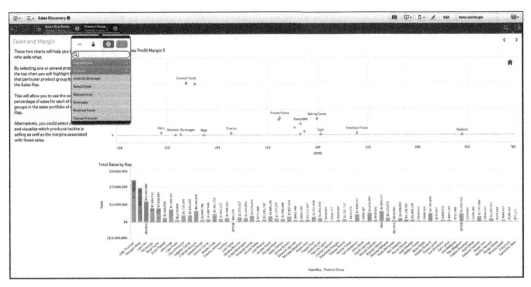

What products are they selling?

Analyzing customer sales

Navigating back to the **Top Customers** sheet, we can see from which customers these sales are generated. Perhaps, while working with these sales representatives, additional promotions can be developed to expand the sales of products such as **Canned Products** to these customers.

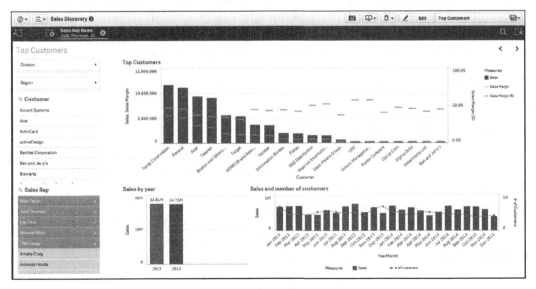

Who are they selling to?

The final area to help improve sales representative performance is to analyze where these products are being sold. In the **US Regional Analysis** sheet, we can see that **Sales by State**, **Customers**, and **Ships to** are nicely dispersed, and additional information is not necessary for the next step:

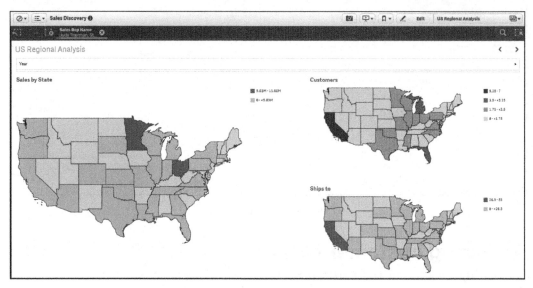

What regions are they selling to?

As you can see, the **Sales Discovery** application provides a 360-degree view of a sales analysis. This is primarily driven by Qlik's associative indexing engine that drives all Qlik-based applications. Additionally, like most analysis processes, the path to discovery of new information cannot be prestaged but rather unfolds based on the next question asked. This is where Qlik Sense excels in enabling a level of interaction with data to drive insight and is only limited by the data that is available. Now, let's turn our attention to how this application was built.

Building the application

Let's start our review of the heart of a Qlik Sense application, the data model. As you can see from the following screenshot, there are twelve tables in the **Sales Discovery** associative model. At the heart of this application is the SalesDetails table. All these tables were created through **Data Load Editor**, which was covered in *Chapter 7, Creating Engaging Applications*. It is worth noting that Qlik and Qlik partners provide both general-purpose connectors and specialized connectors to access a broad array of data sources.

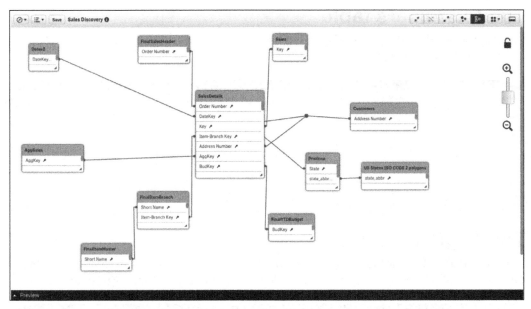

The Sales Discovery model

Let's dig a bit deeper into the key tables. The key tables that drive this application are covered in the following sections.

The SalesDetails table

The `SalesDetails` table contains all the key information about the sales transaction for a specific order. This includes information such as the order number, date, and so on, as shown in the following screenshot:

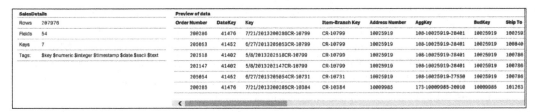

The SalesDetails table

The Customers table

The `Customers` table contains all the key information about the customer: channel, region, account management, and so on:

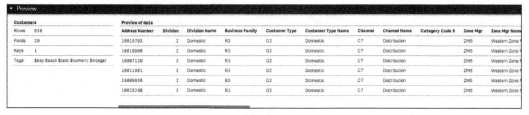

The Customers table

The AggSales table

The `AggSales` table contains all the sales KPI information and is associated with the model so that sales information is available by customer, product, region, and so on:

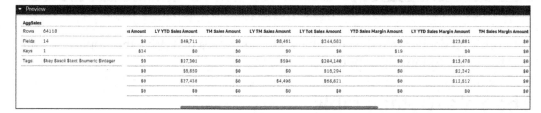

The AggSales table

US States ISO CODE 2 polygons

The `US States ISO CODE 2 polygons` table drives the map visualization in the **US Regional Analysis** sheet. The key field is defined by the state, which drives the associative sections, and the field `US States_Area` is an imported **Keyhole Markup Language** (KML) file that contains the map geographic information. This is stored as blob data in the model, and the map object interprets this information when used in a sheet. This table is shown in the following screenshot:

The US States ISO CODE 2 polygons table

Analyzing the Sales Discovery Library

Now let's turn our attention to what has been exposed in the Sales Discovery Library by the developer to facilitate the creation and sharing of personal sheets.

Dimensions

In the next screenshot, we can see the dimensions that were created. One particular dimension that needs attention is the **Region > Cust** dimension, which provides a drill-down navigation from **Region Name** to **Customer**. This capability usually requires extensive modeling or complex scripts in other BI software products, but with Qlik Sense, this is a simple selection process when creating a dimension. This is another example of the power of Qlik's associative indexing engine in action, but this time, easing the development of navigation within the application.

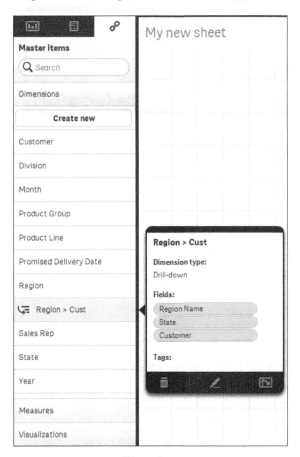

Dimensions

Measures

The next area to cover is **Measures**. These are calculated expressions that most often form the KPIs within an application. We can see in the following screenshot the list of measures that are used and exposed to contributors to allow them to create private sheets. Note that hovering the pointer over any of these objects makes a preview popup appear to provide additional context. In this case, you can see how the measure is calculated. The following screenshot shows **Measures**:

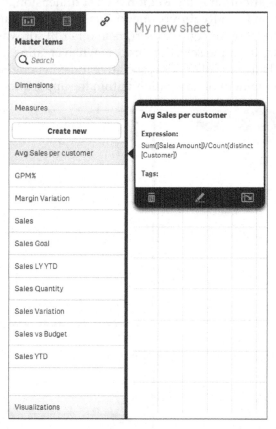

Measures

Additionally, the following table contains the measure definitions that directly tie to the KPIs used in this application:

Measure	Calculation
Avg Sales per customer	*Sum ([Sales Amount]) / Count(distinct [Customer])*
GPM%	*Sum ({<[Product Group Desc] = {*}>}[Sales Margin Amount]) / Sum ({<[Product Group Desc] = {*}>}[Sales Amount])*

Measure	Calculation
Margin Variation	*(Sum ([YTD Sales Margin Amount]) / sum ([LY YTD Sales Margin Amount])) - 1*
Sales	*Sum ([Sales Amount])*
Sales Goal	*Sum ([YTD Budget Amount])*
Sales LY YTD	*Sum ([LY YTD Sales Amount])*
Sales Quantity	*Sum ([Sales Quantity])*
Sales Variation	*(sum ([YTD Sales Amount]) - sum ([LY YTD Sales Amount])) / sum ([LY YTD Sales Amount])*
Sales vs Budget	*Sum ([YTD Sales Amount]) / Sum ([YTD Budget Amount]) - 1*
Sales YTD	*Sum ([YTD Sales Amount])*

Visualizations

The last category of objects in **Library** (**Master items**) is **Visualizations**. These are preformed visualizations that are typically the most popular or requested visualizations. They are defined to help facilitate a user's analysis and can be easily dragged and dropped onto a private sheet. Here, we see a trend line chart for **Number of shipments vs late vs on time**. Each of these visualizations contain predefined dimensions, measures, and chart definitions:

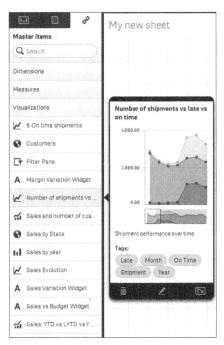

Visualizations

Summary

In summary, Qlik Sense provides unique capabilities to meet the challenging task of analyzing sales data. Without the capabilities offered by Qlik, this task can be difficult due to the size of the data and the many perspectives that can be taken in trying to understand customer buying habits, sales representative productivity, and the responsive nature of the organization in meeting customer needs. Qlik's associative indexing engine powers this exploration. This means that meeting these requirements is no longer challenging at all.

In the next chapter, we will explore how Qlik Sense will meet the needs of Human Resource Discovery.

10
Human Resource Discovery

Just like the previous chapter, this chapter will show you how to apply Qlik® Sense to the challenges of analyzing real data. This chapter's example and many others are available for you to explore on `http://sense-demo.qlik.com`. Again, make sure you bookmark this link, as more demonstrations and examples are constantly being added and updated.

This chapter is about the analysis of Human Resources data, and it covers the following topics:

- General information about common KPIs
- What a typical data model could look like
- An example of how to use the global selector
- Examples of dimensions and measures

The business problem

The term Human Resources analysis covers a wide area of KPIs that use data from a number of different data sources.

It could be that you want to analyze in-house data, for example, the efficiency of the recruitment process and the costs tied to it. It could just as well be analysis of external data, for example, different employee surveys or sentiment analysis on social media.

Just to give you an idea, we have compiled a list of some of the most common areas to investigate when preparing a Human Resources analysis:

- **Recruitment**: This measures the efficiency of the recruitment process; for example, what is the recruitment cost per employee? What is the average lead time to recruit?

- **Employee satisfaction and retention**: This measures employee loyalty; for example, what is the average satisfaction (as measured by a survey)? What is the employee turnover?

- **Training**: This covers the following questions as examples: what is the total expenditure on training? What percent of the employees have gone through the training? What is the number of training hours per employee?

- **Health and Safety**: This covers the following questions as examples: what is the number of accidents per year? How many employees are of adequate health and get safety training? How much are health and safety prevention costs?

- **Career and Compensation**: These cover the following questions as examples: what is the average salary rate? How does it compare to the national average? How much are the salary costs compared to the sales turnover? What is the cost of social and medical insurances?

All of the preceding KPIs can be split by a dimension, month, department, position, tenure, age, and so on.

It might be that you don't have data for all the preceding KPIs, but we can assure you that if you do, you will find it worthwhile to analyze them.

Application features

On our demo site, we have a human resource app. You can find it on `http://sense-demo.qlik.com`, by clicking on the **Human Capital Management** link. In it, you will find a subset of what you can analyze in HR data. Mainly, it analyzes training investments and employee satisfaction.

When you open the app, you will first see the app overview, with a small description of the app and a thumbnail in the form of a small bar chart, as shown in the following screenshot:

The overview of the Human Capital Management application

Below this overview, you will see a number of sheets. These are created according to the dashboard analysis report principles described in *Chapter 4, Overview of a Qlik Sense Application's Life Cycle*. This means that the leftmost sheet is an overview, very much like a dashboard, whereas the other sheets are prepared for analysis and detailed information.

If you click on the Stories button to the left, you will see that the app also contains one story — a story that can be used to present the data in the app. It can also be used as an introduction to the app the first time you open it.

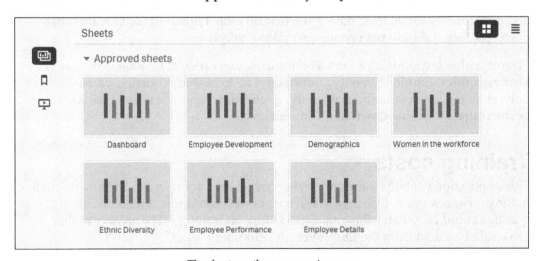

The sheets on the app overview page

Sheets

The first sheet is called **Dashboard**, and if you open this, you will see several key numbers, a couple of charts, and a map. This overview is designed so that you can quickly get a brief understanding of the information without having to make any selections.

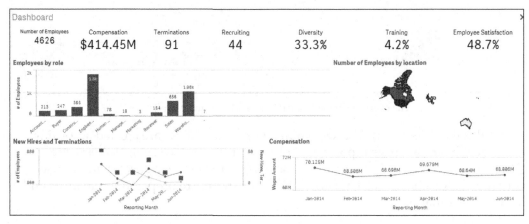

The first sheet – Dashboard

The top-left chart and the map show the number of employees per role and per country. The two bottom charts show the number of hires, number of terminations, and total compensation over time. Note that this sheet does not contain any filter panes because it should not encourage making selections.

The other sheets contain more detailed information, ordered by topics, such as **Demographics**, **Ethnic Diversity**, and so on. The final sheet contains a table only, showing the details about what the application captures, should the user be interested in drilling down to the lowest level.

Training costs

This application contains information that covers only some of the KPIs mentioned in the previous section. One area that it covers well is training. Hence, our first question could be, what is the total expenditure on training? The answer to this can easily be found from the **Employee Development** sheet.

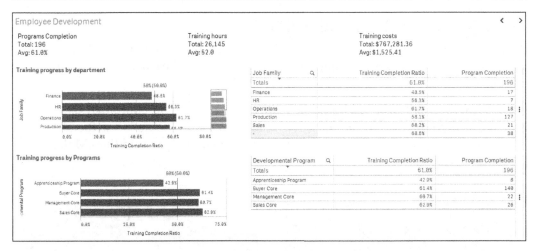

The Employee Development sheet

In the top-right part of the sheet, you can find a textbox containing **Total:** under **Training costs**.

The next question is, what is the percentage of employees who have gone through the training? The answer to this can be found from the same sheet. All charts on this sheet show the training completion ratio, split per department or program. By clicking on a chart, you can drill down to the data and explore how the numbers vary between departments, programs, job, course type, and course name.

When you analyze data in a Qlik Sense application, you will realize that there are many ways of using it. For example, say that you want to look at the training progress by gender, to see whether there is any difference between men and women. You have already found the charts showing training progress on the **Employee Development** sheet, but these only show the progress by department and by program.

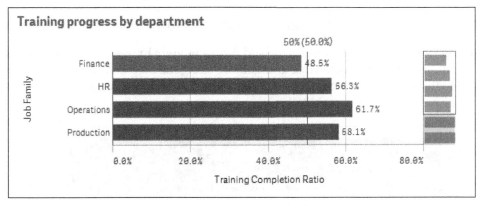

Chart showing training progress by department

Using the global selector

If you have been authorized to create your own visualizations, you can simply go to edit mode, drag **Gender** onto the chart, and replace the existing dimension with **Gender**.

Even if you aren't allowed to change anything, you can still do your analysis. You just have to do it in a different way. What you could then do is use the global selector (to the right in the Selections bar) to select **Female** first, and then **Male**, shown as follows:

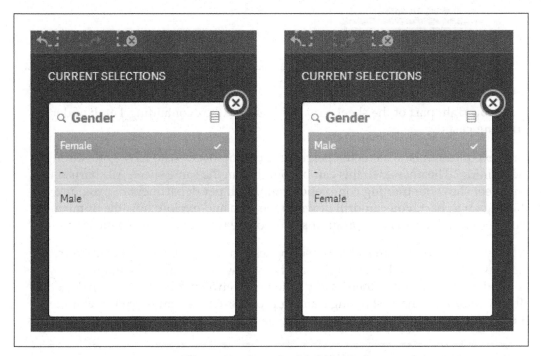

Selecting Gender in the global selector

When you now close the global selector and return to your **Employee Development** sheet, you can toggle between **Male** and **Female** using the Step back and Step forward buttons to the left in the selections bar, as shown in the following screenshot. There's also a Clear all selections button in this bar:

The left part of the Selections bar, with the Step back, Step forward, and Clear all selections buttons

This way, you can see how the chart changes as you toggle between the data of male and female employees.

The next question could be about employee compensation. For this, you need to go to the **Employee Performance** sheet. Here, you will find a table showing all employees and the compensation attached to them. By clicking on **Avg Compensation:** in the **Total / Avg Salary by employee rating** chart, you can sort the employees in ascending or descending order, and can thus get a good overview of the span.

As users, we would probably also want to see a chart showing the average and total salary costs, split by department, but unfortunately, this has not been created by the app developer. However, in a real-life situation, a user should be empowered to create such charts. After all, it is impossible for an application developer to foresee all the needs of a user. Hence, this is a good example of the need for self-service data discovery.

How the application was developed

The data model for the **Human Capital Management** application looks like what is shown in the following screenshot:

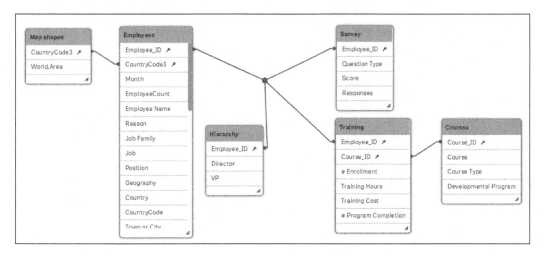

There are six tables in this application:

- Employees: This is the main table, which has one record per employee and month. It contains all of the relevant information about the employee such as country, position, salary, and so on. It would probably be possible to normalize this table into one table containing employee information that doesn't change over time and another table with the time-dependent information.

  However, since the Qlik® engine analyzes the data just as efficiently either way, we don't see any great benefit in spending time structuring the data more.

Employees		Preview of data								
Rows	5219	Employee_ID	CountryCode3	Month	EmployeeCount	Employee Name	Reason	Job Family	Job
Fields	34	231	GBR	Jun-2014	1	Aaron Cohen	Import created action	Production	Engineering
Keys	2	1298	CAN	Jun-2014	2	Abigail Kennedy	*New Job	Operations	Buyer
Tags:	$key $numeric $integer $geoname $ascii $text	1192	USA	Jun-2014	3	Abram Ruiz	Existing Position	Operations	Receiver
		49	USA	Jun-2014	4	Ada Morales	Existing Position	Production	Warehouse
		1013	CAN	Jun-2014	5	Adam Garrison	Existing Position	Sales	Sales
		720	GBR	Jun-2014	6	Adara Cruz	Import created action	Production	Warehouse

Preview of the Employees table

- Hierarchy: This table contains information about the manager of the employee.

- Survey: This table contains the results from an external survey made on employee satisfaction. Such surveys are usually made once in a year, so if the results from several surveys are kept in this table, the key needs to hold information not only about the employee, but also about the year in which the survey was made.

- Training: This table contains information about the training sessions attended. Hence, if an employee has attended two courses, two records are stored. The table also contains costs associated with the training sessions.

- Courses: The possible courses are stored in this separate table.

- Map shapes: This table lists all countries. It has one record per country and could, in principle, hold demographic information about the country. However, in this case, it only holds the map information — the shapes of the countries — used in the map object, which is in the user interface.

Note that this application has fields used for measures in several tables: salary can be found in the Employees table, cost for training can be found in the Training table, and ratings from the survey can be found in the Survey table. This is in sharp contrast to classic BI tools, where all such facts need to be in one single table — the Facts table.

Dimensions

There are many fields that can be used as dimensions, and a large number of them have been added as dimensions to **Library** such as **Employee Name**, **Age Group**, **Department**, and so on.

In principle, any field that a user would be able to use as a grouping symbol should be added as a dimension. However, you should not add cryptic keys or numbers that could be used as measures.

The dimensions in Library

Measures

A number of measures have also been defined, for example, **# of Employees**, **# of Women**, **Attrition**, **# of New Hires**, **Avg Compensation**, and so on.

It is important that the app developer writes the formula correctly, since this is something that could be difficult for a business user. A business user doesn't always have knowledge about the data model, which is something you need in order to get all the expressions right.

In the following table, you can find some of the measures defined in this app:

Measure	Definition
# of Employees	*Count(DISTINCT [EmployeeCount])*
# of Women	*Count ({<[Gender] = {'Female'}>} DISTINCT EmployeeCount)*
Attrition	*Count ({<[Terminated Employee] = {'1'}>} DISTINCT [EmployeeCount])*
Avg Compensation	*Avg([Salary])*
Completed Training ratio	*Sum([# Program Completion]) / Count(DISTINCT EmployeeCount)*
Employee Satisfaction Ratio	*Avg(Score)*
New Hires ratio	*(Count ({< [New Hires] = {'1'} >} DISTINCT EmployeeCount) / Count(DISTINCT EmployeeCount))*
Terminations	*Count ({< [Terminated Employee] = {'1'} >} DISTINCT EmployeeCount)*
Wages Amount	*Sum(Salary)*

Finally, there are also a number of visualizations added to **Library**. These are important, as they help a business user in the initial use of the app.

The most common bar charts and tree maps have been stored here: **Number of employees by role**, **Number of employees by management position**, and so on.

The list of visualizations in Library

Summary

In summary, the analysis of human resource data is easy when you use Qlik Sense's unique capabilities. Such an analysis can otherwise be difficult due to multiple and disparate data sources holding human resource data. Qlik's associative indexing engine powers this exploration, and analysis is made easy for the user.

In the next chapter, we will look at how Qlik Sense can be used to analyze costs, or more specifically, travel expenses.

11
Travel Expense Discovery

The goal of this chapter is to continue our exploration of Qlik® Sense with real data, and how it meets the needs of business discovery in your organization. The Qlik Sense application chosen for this chapter is a topic near and dear to most finance departments: **Travel Expense Management**. Like all the applications covered in this book, please feel free to explore this application live at `http://sense-demo.qlik.com`. With that said, let's turn our attention to the following challenge of travel expense management and how Qlik Sense addresses this common business challenge.

In this chapter, we will cover the following topics:

- Common travel expense analysis challenges
- The unique way Qlik Sense addresses these challenges
- How the application was built

The business problem

Expenses are a major line item of every global company. Traveling cost is a part of every sales and service cycle. Unfortunately, most expense tools capture the transaction but do little to help gain insights about how the expenses were spent, when, and most importantly how, to reduce these expenses when possible. Some key questions can include:

- How are expenses tracked verses budget?
- What is the actual amount spent to date?
- What is our largest expense type?
- How can we reduce expenses?

Application features

Now let's take a look at the unique way Qlik Sense approaches solving the business problems mentioned in the previous section. Qlik Sense's associative model allows users to answer common questions through filters, but they can also address the more important follow up questions that arise. As you may recall, this type of analysis uses "The Power of Gray", named after the color Qlik Sense assigns to nonassociated elements (potential opportunities for improvement) highlighted in *Chapter 5, Empowering Next Generation Data Discovery Consumers*.

Key questions can include:

- How are expenses tracked verses budget?
- What is actual amount spent till date?
- Is my department over budget?
- What is our largest expense variance?
- What is the meal expense breakdown?
- How can we reduce expenses?

Before we begin, let's review the main sheets within the **Travel Expense Management** application. As noted in the following screenshot, the application is made of three sheets: **Dashboard**, **Airfare**, and **Food Expenses**:

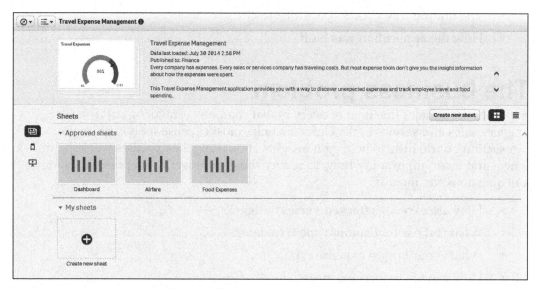

The Travel Expense Management overview

These sheets provide insights into the overall expense management, and the two largest expense categories of airfare and food. With that said, let's now turn our attention to our first question.

Tracking expenses

A key question is how to manage departmental expenses on a quarterly basis. How are expenses tracked versus what has been budgeted?

In the following screenshot, we can see in the sample application that **Total Expenses** is below budget by $30,964. This is good news. Additionally, we see that the largest expense is **Airfare**, and what is more troubling is that **Food Expenses** is running $6,679 over budget.

How are expenses tracked versus budget?

Analyzing expenses overspend

Taking a closer look at food expenses such as breakfast, lunch, and dinner, we can see that for most of 2013 (11 out of 12 months), employees spent more for meals than was budgeted. Exploring a little deeper, we can see that as you'd expect, **Dinner** takes up the majority of the expenses with $30,735. What's more interesting is that the budget to actual variance starts to sharply grow in May, October, and November.

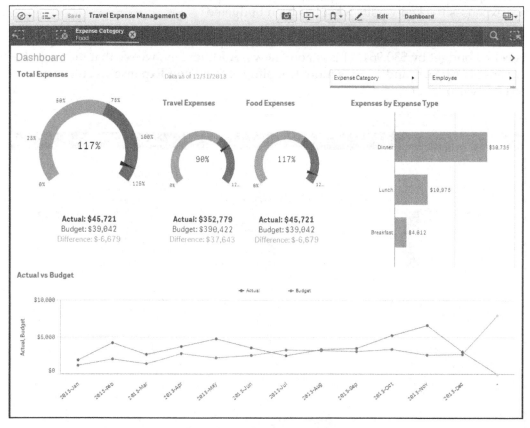

What is the meal expense breakdown?

Now that we have highlighted a problem with food expenses, let's start to use the more detailed information that is available in the **Food Expenses** sheet, shown in the next screenshot. Additional external information is always helpful in variance analysis. In the following screenshot, we can see not only **Average Employee Daily Meal Expenses vs Average US Per Diem Meal Rates (external source)**, but also **Average Employee Daily Meal Expenses vs Average US Per Diem Meal Rates (external source) by Employee** on a monthly basis:

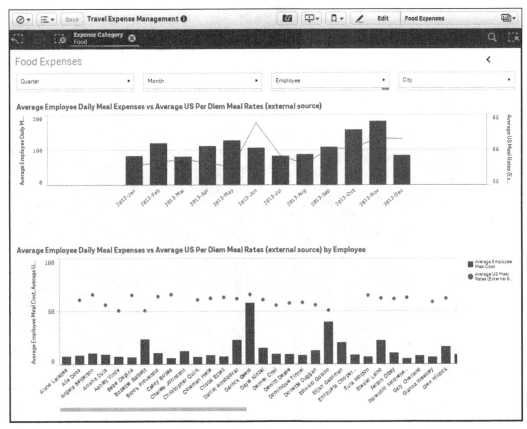

What is the Average Employee expense verses Average US Meals expenses?

Digging deeper into the data

Overall, the company seems to be performing well against the US average, but let's dig a bit deeper. For example, are there employees that do not spend on meals, which could be lowering the company average? To find this out, simply select the global filter (also known as the Selections tool) icon, as shown in the following screenshot:

Global filter

Using "The Power of Gray" (nonassociated elements), we can see in the **Employee** dimension that four employees do not spend on their meals, as shown in the following screenshot:

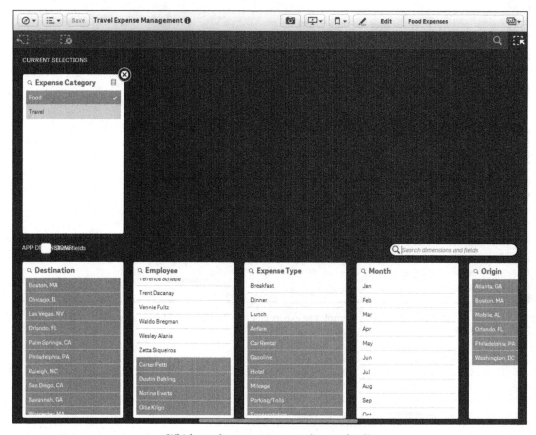

Which employees are not spending on food?

Knowing this, we can exit the global filter screen and continue our employee meal analysis. What started off as a travel expense analysis has, through Qlik Sense, narrowed down the analysis to an employee meal analysis. As we scroll through the employees, as shown in the following screenshot, we immediately get to an employee (**Ileen Menard**) who has exceeded the average US per diem allowance significantly, and by selecting **Ileen Menard**, you can see that May was the month with the significant variance:

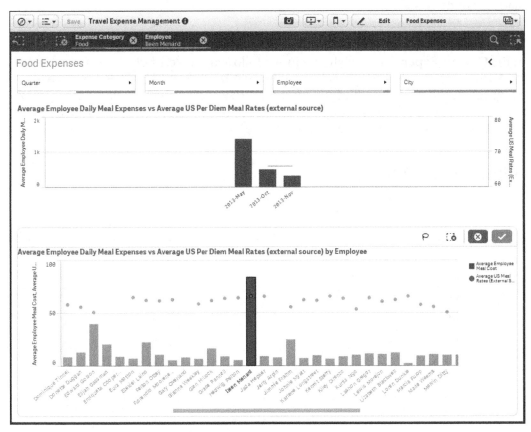

Which employee exceeds the average for US Meals per diem?

Creating an analysis story for travel expenses

Now that we've completed our analysis, let's create a **Travel Expense Analysis** story so that we can share our findings through our organization.

In *Chapter 6, Contributing to Data Discovery*, we reviewed the role of a contributor, and how to create a Qlik Sense story and publish it so that others may view their analysis. Based on the analysis discussed in the previous section, the travel expense story is made up of three sheets.

Creating an overview

In the **Overall Expenses** sheet shown in the following screenshot, you can see the **In 2013, the company overall stayed below budget by almost $31,000. While Travel expenses were well below budget, food expenses were $6,679 above budget (17%)** annotation as well as the key snapshot gauges of the actual to budget performance total, **Travel Expenses**, and **Food Expenses**:

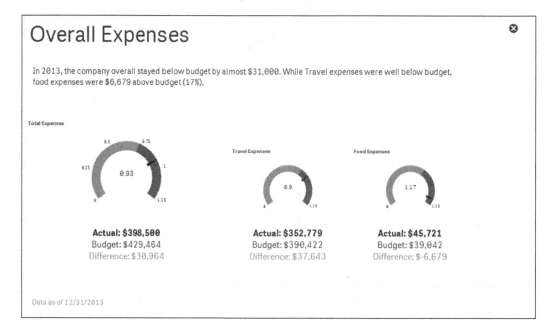

Sharing our analysis

Now that the overview of the analysis is complete, let's move on the next step and share what was found in analyzing **Food Expenses**. The **Food Expenses** story sheet, shown in the following screenshot, highlights that for most of 2013 (11 out of 12 months), employees spent more for meals than was budgeted:

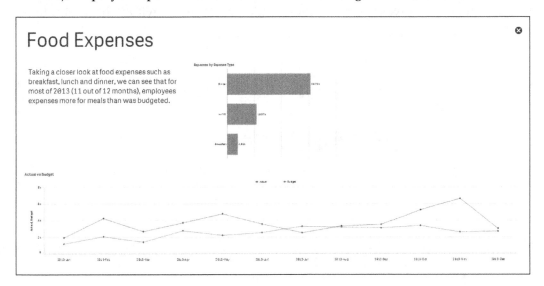

Finishing the story

With these two story sheets defined, a final sheet for the story will require a bit more interaction for the viewer. As noted in *Chapter 6, Contributing to Data Discovery*, this is achieved by embedding the **Food Expenses** sheet directly into the story, as shown in the following screenshot. This will allow the author to not only narrate the findings but also invite the viewer to explore these findings and others within the application:

With the story created, the final annotation makes the following recommendation: **As a company, we should consider increasing the budget for meal expenses. Most of our employees expensed less that the per diem rate in 2013 and were significantly above budget in their meal expenses so increasing the budget seems like a good idea.**

Now that we have covered the application features, let's turn our attention to how it was built.

Developing the application

Let's start our review of the heart of a Qlik Sense application: the data model. As you can see from the following screenshot, there are six tables in the **Travel Expense Management** associative model. At the heart of this application is the Expenses table. These tables were created through **Data Load Editor**, which was covered in *Chapter 7, Creating Engaging Applications*. It is worth noting that Qlik and Qlik partners provide both general-purpose connectors and specialized connectors to access a broad array of data sources.

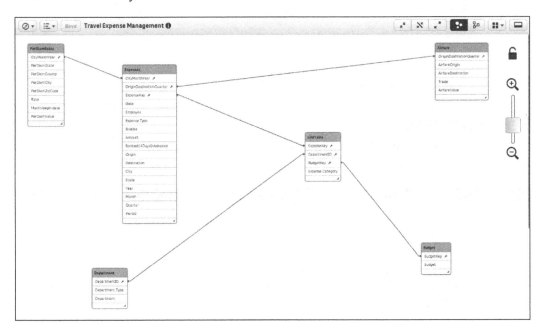

Examining the key tables

Let's examine the key tables.

Expenses

The Expenses table contains all the key information (shown in the following screenshot) about the expense transaction of an employee. This includes information such as the date, employee name, expense type, and so on.

Expenses		Preview of data					
Rows	10527	CityMonthYear	OriginDestinationQuarter	ExpenseKey	Date	Employee	Expense Type
Fields	17	Las Vegas_Oct_2013	_Q4	Food_101_10/1/2013	10/17/2013	Angela Betterton	Breakfast
Keys	3	Las Vegas_Oct_2013	_Q4	Food_101_10/1/2013	10/17/2013	Angela Betterton	Dinner
Tags:	$key $ascii $text $numeric $integer $timestamp $date	Las Vegas_Oct_2013	_Q4	Food_101_10/1/2013	10/17/2013	Angela Betterton	Dinner
		Las Vegas_Oct_2013	_Q4	Food_101_10/1/2013	10/17/2013	Angela Betterton	Dinner
		Philadelphia_Nov_2013	_Q4	Food_101_11/1/2013	11/7/2013	Angela Betterton	Breakfast
		Philadelphia_Nov_2013	_Q4	Food_101_11/1/2013	11/7/2013	Angela Betterton	Breakfast

The Expenses table

PerDiemRates

The PerDiemsRates table contains all the key information (shown in the following screenshot) about state, city, month, rates, and so on:

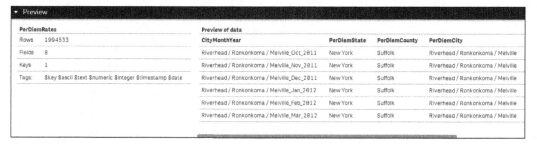

PerDiemRates		Preview of data			
Rows	1994533	CityMonthYear	PerDiemState	PerDiemCounty	PerDiemCity
Fields	8	Riverhead / Ronkonkoma / Melville_Oct_2011	New York	Suffolk	Riverhead / Ronkonkoma / Melville
Keys	1	Riverhead / Ronkonkoma / Melville_Nov_2011	New York	Suffolk	Riverhead / Ronkonkoma / Melville
Tags:	$key $ascii $text $numeric $integer $timestamp $date	Riverhead / Ronkonkoma / Melville_Dec_2011	New York	Suffolk	Riverhead / Ronkonkoma / Melville
		Riverhead / Ronkonkoma / Melville_Jan_2012	New York	Suffolk	Riverhead / Ronkonkoma / Melville
		Riverhead / Ronkonkoma / Melville_Feb_2012	New York	Suffolk	Riverhead / Ronkonkoma / Melville
		Riverhead / Ronkonkoma / Melville_Mar_2012	New York	Suffolk	Riverhead / Ronkonkoma / Melville

The PerDiemRates table

Airfare

The `Airfare` table contains all the key information (shown in the following screenshot) about the origin, destination, airfare value, and so on:

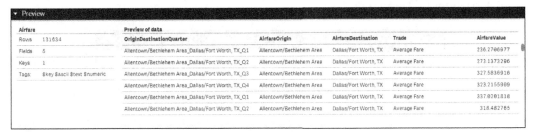

The Airfare table

Department

The `Department` table contains all the key information (shown in the following screenshot) about the department ID, type, and department name:

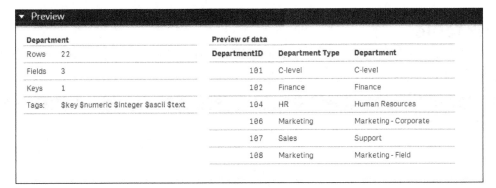

The Department table

Budget

The Budget table contains all the key information (shown in the following screenshot) about the budgeted amount using a compound key value that includes the expense type, department ID, and date:

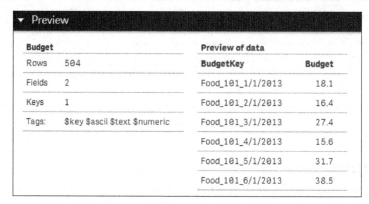

The Budget table

LinkTable

The LinkTable table contains all the keys (shown in the following screenshot) to link the expense, department, and budget tables:

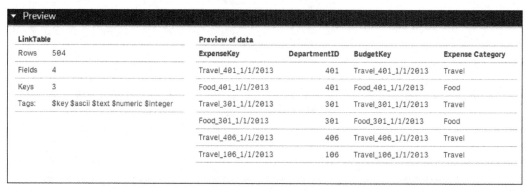

The LinkTable table

Dimensions

Now let's turn our attention to what has been exposed in the Travel Expense Library by the developer to facilitate the creation and sharing of personal sheets. In the following screenshot, we can see the dimensions that were created. One particular dimension that is worth calling out is the **Expense** dimension, which provides a drill navigation from **ExpenseCategory** to **ExpenseType**. This capability usually requires extensive modeling or complex scripts in other BI software products, but with Qlik Sense, this is a simple selection process when creating the dimension. This is another example of the power of Qlik's associative indexing engine in action, but this time, easing the development of navigation within the application.

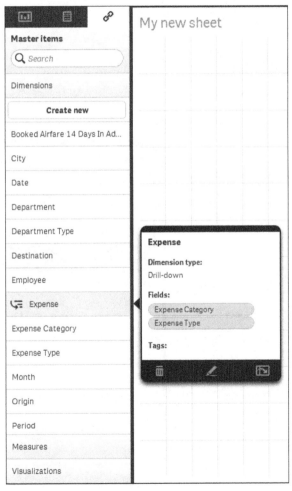

Dimensions

Measures

The next area to cover is **Measures**. These are calculated expressions that most often form the KPIs within an application. In the following screenshot, we can see a list of measures that are used and exposed to contributors to allow them to create private sheets. Note that hovering the pointer over any of these objects makes a preview popup appear to provide additional context. In this case, you can see how the measure **Actual - Food** is calculated.

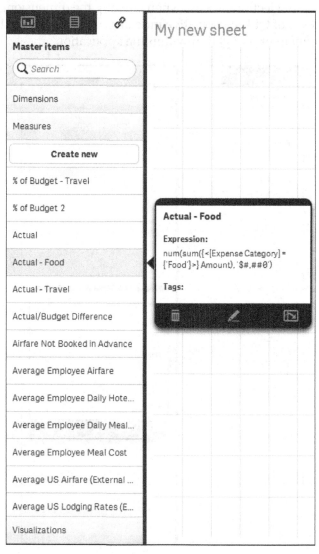

Measures

Additionally, the following table contains the measure definitions that directly tie to the KPIs used in this application. Please refer to the Qlik Sense online help for additional information on the Qlik Sense function, which is available at `https://help.qlik.com`.

The measure expressions include:

Measure	Calculation
% of Budget - Travel	*num(sum({<[Expense Category] = {'Travel'}>} Amount)* */ sum({<[Expense Category] = {'Travel'}>} Budget), '#,##0%')*
% of Budget 2	*num((Sum(Budget)/sum(Amount))-1, '#,##0%')Amount])*
Actual	*Num(Sum(Amount),'$#,##0')*
Actual - Food	*num(sum({<[Expense Category] = {'Food'}>} Amount), '$#,##0')*
Actual - Travel	*num(sum({<[Expense Category] = {'Travel'}>} Amount), '$#,##0')*
Actual/Budget Difference	*Num(Sum(Budget)-Sum(Amount),'$#,##0')*
Airfare Not Booked in Advance	*Num(Avg({<[Expense Type]={'Airfare'}, Booked14DaysInAdvance={'No'}>} Amount),'$#,##0.00')*
Average Employee Airfare	*Avg({<[Expense Type]={'Airfare'}>} Amount)*
Average Employee Daily Hotel Cost	*Sum({<[Expense Type]={'Hotel'}>} Amount)/ Count(DISTINCT Employee)*
Average Employee Daily Meal Cost	*Sum({<[Expense Type]={'Breakfast', 'Lunch', 'Dinner'}>} Amount)/Count(DISTINCT Employee)*
Average US Airfare (External Source)	*Avg({<Trade={'Average Fare'}>} AirfareValue)*
Average US Lodging Rates (External Source)	*Avg({<Rate={'Lodging'}>} PerDiemValue)*
Average US Meal Rates (External Source)	*Avg({<Rate={'M&IE'}>} PerDiemValue)*
Avg Airfare - Largest Carrier (External Source)	*Avg({<Trade={'Average Fare - Largest Carrier'}>} AirfareValue)*
Avg Airfare - Low Fare Carrier (External Source)	*Avg({<Trade={'Average Fare - Low Fare Carrier'}>} AirfareValue)*

Measure	Calculation
Booked Airfare in Advance	*Num(Avg({<[Expense Type]={'Airfare'}, Booked14DaysInAdvance={'Yes'}>} Amount),'\$#,##0.00')*
Booked Difference	*Num(Avg({<[Expense Type]={'Airfare'}, Booked14DaysInAdvance={'Yes'}>} Amount)-Avg({<[Expense Type]={'Airfare'}, Booked14DaysInAdvance={'No'}>} Amount),'\$#,##0.00')*
Booked Difference %	*Num((Avg({<[Expense Type]={'Airfare'}, Booked14DaysInAdvance={'Yes'}>} Amount)/Avg({<[Expense Type]={'Airfare'}, Booked14DaysInAdvance={'No'}>} Amount))-1,'#,##0.00%')*
Budget	*Num(Sum(Budget),'\$#,##0')*
Budget - Food	*num(sum({<[Expense Category] = {'Food'}>} Budget), '\$#,##0')*
Budget - Travel	*num(sum({<[Expense Category] = {'Travel'}>} Budget), '\$#,##0')*
Food Difference	*num(sum({<[Expense Category] = {'Food'}>} Budget)-sum({<[Expense Category] = {'Food'}>} Amount), '\$#,##0')*
Travel Difference	*num(sum({<[Expense Category] = {'Travel'}>} Budget)-sum({<[Expense Category] = {'Travel'}>} Amount), '\$#,##0')*

Visualizations

The last category of objects in the **Library** (**Master items**) is **Visualizations**. These are preformed visualizations that are typically the most popular or requested. They are defined to help facilitate a user's analysis and can be easily dragged and dropped onto a private sheet. In the following screenshot, we see a horizontal bar chart that analyzes the variance in **Booked Airfare in Advance vs Not in Advance**. Each of these visualizations contains predefined dimensions, measures, and chart definitions.

The Travel Expense visualizations

Summary

In summary, Qlik Sense provides unique capabilities to meet the challenging task of analyzing and managing travel expenses. Without the capabilities offered by Qlik, this task can be difficult due to the size of the data and the many perspectives that can be taken in trying to understand airline purchasing, meal expense habits, and the impact on meeting corporate budget requirements. Qlik's associative indexing engine powers this exploration and means that meeting these requirements is no longer challenging at all.

In the next chapter, we will explore how Qlik Sense meets the needs of demographic data discovery.

12
Demographic Data Discovery

In this final chapter, we shall finish our exploration of real data with Qlik Sense by moving beyond the standard structures of the office and showing the full possibilities of the software for analysis of almost any kind of imaginable data. We'll therefore be looking at applying Qlik Sense to demographic data. As before, this example and many others are available for you to explore at http://sense-demo.qlik.com.

This chapter will cover the aspects necessary for demographic data discovery, including:

- General information about common KPIs
- Examples showing how to use the lasso selection in maps and scatter charts
- Examples of dimensions and measures

The problem analysis

With Qlik Sense, it is possible to analyze not only business data, but rather *any* data. One great example is demographic data—statistics of countries and regions on anything from age and gender to income and life expectancy.

Such data can be found on a number of Internet sites and downloaded for your convenience, for example, from the following websites:

- United Nations (https://data.un.org)
- Federal government of the United States (www.data.gov)
- European Union (http://ec.europa.eu/eurostat)

Demographic data is used and analyzed as is by a number of nongovernmental organizations that need it for their activities. The common measures required are GDP per capita, population, unemployment rate, inflation, life expectancy, happiness, trade balance, labor cost, national debt, election results, and so on.

Often, interesting questions about correlations are asked; for example, how does happiness correlate with material standards and health? How is the population growth and number of children affected by factors such as life expectancy, poverty, and average salary? How has life expectancy improved over the years? If you haven't seen Hans Rosling's presentations on the Internet on this topic, we strongly recommend them. They show that data analysis is both important and fun.

Common dimensions in demographic data are country, region, gender, age group, ethnicity, and so on. An example can be seen in the following graph, where you can see life expectancy and per capita GDP for different countries. Many developing countries are found in the lower-left quadrant, whereas the richer countries usually are found in the upper-right quadrant.

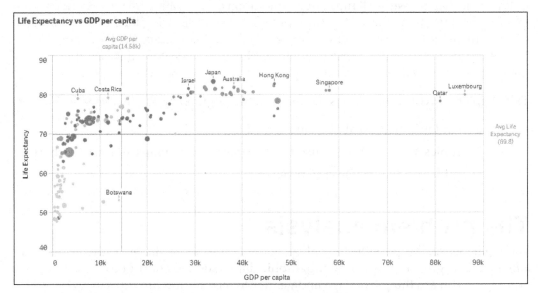

Life expectancy versus per capita GDP

You can clearly see that the two numbers are highly correlated. The higher the GDP, the higher the life expectancy.

These measures can often be linked to your business data as well, to enable a deeper understanding of your data. For instance, you can divide your country sales by the population of the country, thereby getting a relative sales number, which tells you how well you sell in that country. Or if you assume that the market space in the country is roughly proportional to the GDP, you can divide your sales by the GDP and use this number to compare market penetration between countries.

These numbers will answer questions such as, "How well are we selling in this country, given the potential?".

Application features

On our demo site, we have an app with a number of demographic measures per country. You can find it at http://sense-demo.qlik.com under the name **Happiness**. It analyzes, among other demographic indexes, the **Happy Planet Index (HPI)** in a number of countries. You can learn more about this index at www.happyplanetindex.org.

This index measures the sustainable well-being of 151 countries across the globe, focusing not on their abilities to produce material goods and services, but rather on their abilities to produce long, happy, and sustainable lives for the people who live in them. A happy life doesn't have to come at the expense of our environment, and the HPI is used to promote a policy that puts the well-being of people and the planet first.

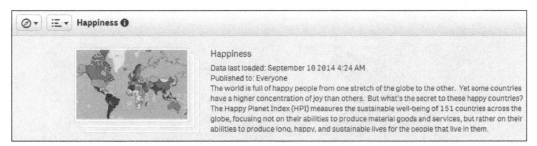

The app overview of the Happiness application

Below this overview, you will see a number of sheets. The leftmost sheet is an introduction, whereas the other sheets are prepared for analysis and detailed information.

If you click on the Stories button to the left, you will see that the app also contains one story—a story that can be used to present data in the app. It can also be used as an introduction to the app the first time you open it.

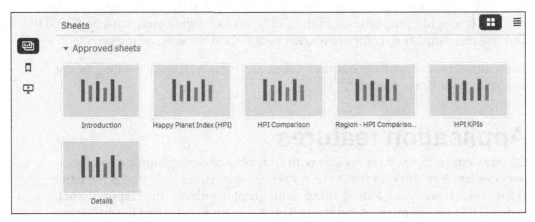

The sheets on the app overview page

The first sheet with charts is called **Happy Planet Index (HPI)**. On it, you will see the happiness index for all countries, first on a map, and then in a table.

The countries in the map are colored according to the happiness index. The darker the color, the higher the index.

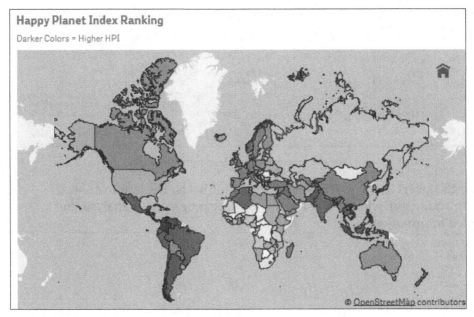

Map showing the happiness index per country

Below the map, there are three scatter charts showing the happiness index per country, plotted against the life expectancy, GDP per capita, and total population. These three charts are excellent tools to analyze any correlation between happiness and the mentioned demographic measures.

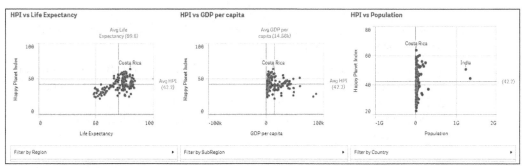

Scatter charts that show the correlation (or lack of correlation) between
happiness and other demographic measures

Finally, at the bottom, you have three filter panes, allowing the user to choose only a region, subregion, or country to zoom in the numbers for a specific area.

The other sheets contain additional and more detailed information, ordered by topics. The final sheet contains a table showing the details, should the user be interested in drilling down to the lowest level.

Analysis

When looking at data in this app, the first question that pops up in the user's mind is usually, "Is there any correlation between happiness and *x*?". To get a qualitative answer to this, you only need to browse through the scatter charts.

On the **Happy Planet Index (HPI)** sheet, you have three scatter charts. In the leftmost chart, **HPI vs Life Expectancy**, you can see a correlation between the two measures, at least for lower life expectancies. In the other two charts, however, there is no clear correlation.

On the **HPI Comparison** sheet, you have three additional scatter charts. In the leftmost chart, **HPI vs Happy Life Years**, you can see a weak correlation between the two measures. The same is true for the rightmost chart, **HPI vs Global Footprint**, but in the chart in the middle (**HPI vs Governance**), there is no clear correlation.

However, as in all of statistics, you have to be careful with your conclusions. Firstly, correlation does not imply causation. You have to look at many factors and use common sense to find the true cause and effect. In this case, it is just that the happiness index is an artificial index calculated from the life expectancy and the ecological footprint among others, hence the correlation.

Using the lasso selector to make selections

Now let's explore the data. One question could be, "Where in the world do we find the countries with a low average life expectancy?" To answer this, you need to make a selection in the scatter chart showing life expectancy:

1. First, maximize the scatter chart by clicking on the Full screen arrow in the upper-right corner of the object.

2. Then click on the chart so that the chart controls, including the lasso symbol, appear in the upper-right corner. Next, click on the Turn on lasso selection option. Now you can draw a line around the points you want to select. Finally, confirm your selection by clicking on the green tick mark in the upper-right corner.

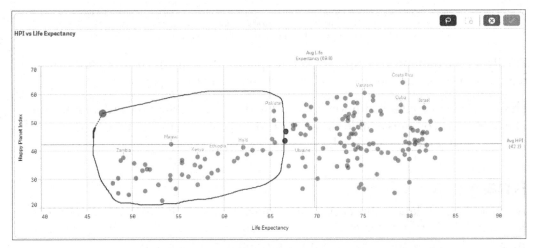

Lasso selection in the scatter chart

If you now look at the map, you will see where these countries appear in the world. It's predominantly Africa and South Asia. If you click on the map, you can zoom in using the scroll wheel of the mouse. You can also pan the map.

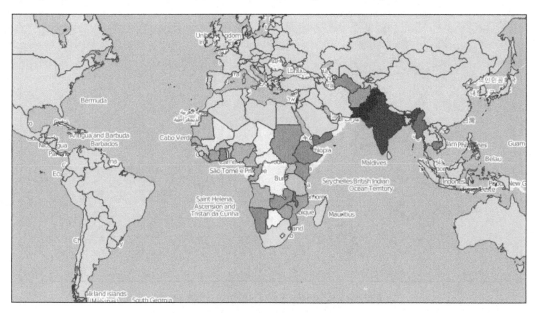

Countries with low life expectancy

Of course, you can also make a selection the other way around. Use the lasso selector in the map and see how the selected countries are distributed in the scatter chart. The way to do this is as follows:

1. Zoom in on the map.
2. Click on the object.
3. Click on the Turn on lasso selection option and encircle the part of the world you want to explore.

4. Finally, confirm your selection.

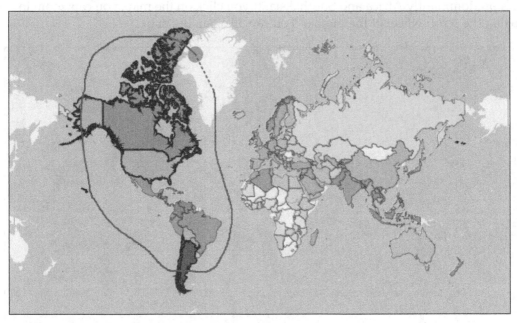

Making a lasso selection of America on the map

Using the global selector to make selections

You can also use the global selector to make selections. If you click on the global selector (to the right in the toolbar with the Selections tool as a popup), you can make selections directly in the fields.

For instance, you may have a question like this: "Where in the world do I find the richest countries?". In such a case, perform the following steps:

1. Open the global selector and find a field called **GDP/capita ($PPP)**. To do this, you first need to check **Show fields** in the global selector.

2. Once you have found this field, you can investigate it just by scrolling. You will then see that there are some countries with less than $400 in GDP per capita, while the richest countries have more than $80,000 in GDP per capita.

If you want to find the countries where the GDP is greater than $10,000, perform the following steps:

1. Click on the listbox and type >10000.

2. Confirm the search by pressing *Enter*, and confirm the selection by clicking on the green tick mark.

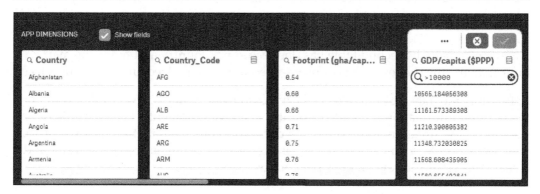

Selecting the countries in the world with the highest GDP

If you now close the global selector and go back to the map and the scatter charts, you will be able to see where you find the richest countries, both on the map and in the scatter charts.

How the application was developed

The data model of the **Happiness** application looks like what is shown in the following screenshot:

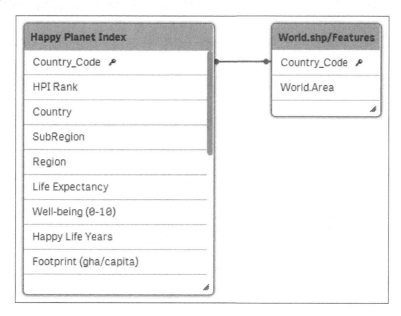

This is an extremely simple data model that only contains one table of real data, `Happy Planet Index`, and an additional table listing all countries, `World.shhp/Features`. The second table has one record per country and holds the map information — the shapes of the country — used in the map object in the user interface.

In this app, the data table has exactly one record per country — a record that contains the relevant information for a given country at a given moment. However, this is not always the situation. More often, the data table contains data for many countries over many points in time, for example, one record per combination of a country and a year. This results in several lines per country.

Dimensions

There are not many fields that can be used as dimensions. The three available fields are region, subregion, and country. The world is split into 7 regions and 19 subregions. A country can only belong to one subregion and one region. These fields have been added to **Library**. In addition, a drill-down dimension has been created from the three fields.

One way of adding dimensions could be by creating "buckets" based on one of the measures, for example, population. Countries could then be grouped under **Large**, **Medium**, and **Small** classes, which would be stored in a new field, **Population Class**.

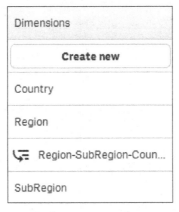

The dimensions in Library

Measures

A number of measures have also been defined, for example, GDP, happiness index, global footprint, life expectancy, and so on.

It is important that the app developer formulates the formulas correctly, since this is something that could be difficult for the business user. The business user doesn't always have knowledge about the data model, which is something you need in order to get all the expressions right.

In the following table, you can find some of the measures defined in this app:

Measure	Definition
GDP per Capita	*Avg([GDP/capita])*
Global Footprint	*Avg([Footprint])*
Governance Rank	*Only[Governance Rank])*
Happy Life Years	*Only([Happy Life Years])*
Happy Planet Index	*Only([Happy Planet Index])*
HPI Rank	*Only([HPI Rank])*
Population	*Only(Population)*

Several of these measures can be defined differently. How you do this is very much a matter of taste. For instance, the measures where the Only() function is used can also be defined using Sum() or Avg(). As long as you only have a single number, all three functions will return the same answer.

But how do you want Qlik Sense to behave when there are several countries, for example, a region that should be represented by one value? For the **Population** measure, the obvious function to use would be Sum(). Then the total population of the region will then be shown.

However, for a rank, you won't want to use Sum() because it would show an incorrect number. You could use Avg(), which would give the average rank between the countries. An average is clearly better, but it is still not mathematically correct. Then it might be better to use Only(), which doesn't return an answer at all when more than one country is involved.

Summary

The analysis of demographic data is easy when you use Qlik Sense. Obviously, this analysis can also be made with a number of other tools, since the data model is very simple. However, with Qlik Sense, it is easy to build further. Qlik's associative indexing engine powers the analysis and ensures that you can develop or change your apps quickly and easily. With Qlik Sense, data discovery and analysis is made easy.

With the end of this chapter, we have also reached the end of the book. We took you from the history of Qlik to how to develop applications, and finally gave you some examples of how applications can look.

We hope that after reading this book, you have acquired some skills that will be useful when you develop your own Qlik Sense applications. We also think you now have a better understanding of the thoughts behind Qlik Sense, and wish you good luck in your endeavors.

Welcome to the community of Qlik users!

Index

measures
adding 102
media library 77, 78
model
assumptions 94
data model 94
data model viewer, using 96
multinode 128

N

Named CAL 130
nodes 127

O

Open Database Connectivity (ODBC) 92
Operations Monitor 140

P

PerDiemRates table, Travel Expense
Discovery 186
pie chart 112
preview mode
using 97
private bookmarks
creating 52-54
private sheet
about 39
creating 55-59
publishing 60-69

Q

Qlik
history 5, 6
Qlik Management Console (QMC) 125
Qlik Sense
about 6
application 27
company culture 6
competition 7
customer requisites 24
demo, URL 145
information activism 26
information, as asset 25
information, as differentiator 25

IT role, elevation 26
IT role, evolution 26
market dynamics 7
market factors 21
modern business 9
Qlik Sense Engine Service (QIX) 124
Qlik Sense Library 50
Qlik Sense Management
Console (QMC) 27
Qlik Sense Proxy Service (QPS) 124
Qlik Sense Repository Database (QRD) 124
Qlik Sense Repository Service (QRS) 124
Qlik Sense Scheduler Service (QSS) 124
Qlik Sense server
access rules 131
connectivity management 137
deploying 128
License Enabling File (LEF) 129
managing 133, 134
monitoring 140
multinode 128, 129
security 141
security, rules 138, 139
single node 128, 129
streams, defining 136
system management 138
tasks 137
tokens 130, 131
user directories 135
users 135
QlikView
about 5
applications, migrating to Qlik Sense 117
QlikView.Next project
about 8
themes 8
QlikView to Qlik Sense, application
migration
about 117
script, changes 117
user interface, changes 118
Qlik way
about 17
calculation, on demand 18, 19
color coding 17
data navigation, freedom 17

Thank you for buying
Learning Qlik® Sense
The Official Guide

About Packt Publishing

Packt, pronounced 'packed', published its first book, *Mastering phpMyAdmin for Effective MySQL Management*, in April 2004, and subsequently continued to specialize in publishing highly focused books on specific technologies and solutions.

Our books and publications share the experiences of your fellow IT professionals in adapting and customizing today's systems, applications, and frameworks. Our solution-based books give you the knowledge and power to customize the software and technologies you're using to get the job done. Packt books are more specific and less general than the IT books you have seen in the past. Our unique business model allows us to bring you more focused information, giving you more of what you need to know, and less of what you don't.

Packt is a modern yet unique publishing company that focuses on producing quality, cutting-edge books for communities of developers, administrators, and newbies alike. For more information, please visit our website at www.packtpub.com.

About Packt Enterprise

In 2010, Packt launched two new brands, Packt Enterprise and Packt Open Source, in order to continue its focus on specialization. This book is part of the Packt Enterprise brand, home to books published on enterprise software – software created by major vendors, including (but not limited to) IBM, Microsoft, and Oracle, often for use in other corporations. Its titles will offer information relevant to a range of users of this software, including administrators, developers, architects, and end users.

Writing for Packt

We welcome all inquiries from people who are interested in authoring. Book proposals should be sent to author@packtpub.com. If your book idea is still at an early stage and you would like to discuss it first before writing a formal book proposal, then please contact us; one of our commissioning editors will get in touch with you.

We're not just looking for published authors; if you have strong technical skills but no writing experience, our experienced editors can help you develop a writing career, or simply get some additional reward for your expertise.

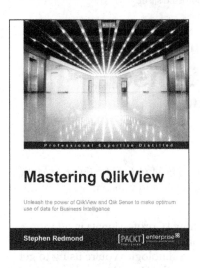

Mastering QlikView

ISBN: 978-1-78217-329-8   Paperback: 422 pages

Unleash the power of QlikView and Qlik Sense to make optimum use of data for Business Intelligence

1. Learn the best ways to load data to optimize the QlikView experience.

2. Display data in a way that is easy to understand for most number of users.

3. Discover advanced expressions and scripting techniques with lots of code and screenshots.

QlikView 11 for Developers

ISBN: 978-1-84968-606-8   Paperback: 534 pages

Develop Business Intelligence applications with QlikView 11

1. Learn to build applications for Business Intelligence while following a practical case -- HighCloud Airlines. Each chapter develops parts of the application and it evolves throughout the book along with your own QlikView skills.

2. The code bundle for each chapter can be accessed on your local machine without having to purchase a QlikView license.

3. The hands-on approach allows you to build a QlikView application that integrates real data from several different sources and presents it in dashboards, analyses and reports.

QlikView Server and Publisher

ISBN: 978-1-78217-985-6   Paperback: 176 pages

Deploy and manage QlikView Server and QlikView Publisher on platforms ranging from a single server to a multiserver clustered environment

1. Learn how to install and utilize the feature-rich QlikView with a step-by-step approach.

2. Configure the appropriate environment for your server implementation.

3. Discover how to shield your QlikView server by implementing third-party security.

4. Share and manage your data using the QlikView Publisher.

QlikView for Developers Cookbook

ISBN: 978-1-78217-973-3   Paperback: 290 pages

Discover the strategies needed to tackle the most challenging task facing the QlikView developer

1. Learn beyond QlikView training.

2. Discover QlikView Advanced GUI development, advanced scripting, complex data modelling issues, and much more.

3. Accelerate the growth of your QlikView developer ability.

4. Based on over 7 years' experience of QlikView development.

Please check **www.PacktPub.com** for information on our titles

CPSIA information can be obtained at www.ICGtesting.com
Printed in the USA
LVOW03s2318250515

439806LV00019B/961/P